RECESSION BUSTERS' BUSINESS BIBLE

By Gerry & Rory Carron

For Kathy

'It is neither the strongest of the species that survives, nor the most intelligent but the one that is most responsive to change.'

Charles Darwin

First published in 2011 by
Gerry Carron
94 Moyne Road,
Ranelagh,
Dublin 6,
Ireland.

ISBN: 978-0-9570945-0-5

Contents:

CHAPTER 1

Introduction

Having started out on the bottom rung of the ladder, by the time I reached the middle rung I was too exhausted to go any further. My advice to the new generation of entrepreneurial people is to start at the top and to give running your own business a shot.

After I graduated in economics, I trained as a chartered accountant for three years in Dublin. My first post-qualification job was in Anglo Irish Bank plc. The activities in this bank later contributed significantly to bursting the Irish economy and could potentially expedite the disintegration of the Eurozone.

In Anglo Irish Bank, I worked closely with the CEO, Sean Fitzpatrick, for several years. I left the bank in 1990 and I will never cease to be amazed that Sean survived for a further 18 years, before the revelations emerged in 2008 that he and some of his colleagues had been 'cooking the books'.

After I left Anglo, I acquired interests in a multitude of different businesses, including hotels, leisure, golf, radio stations and e-money products, both in Ireland and across mainland Europe. Some of these have been very successful whilst others have failed.

Due to my involvement in so many enterprises and with my experience in banking over the years, many business people in financial trouble would contact me seeking guidance on how to resolve their problems. I would receive calls at all hours of the day and night. Often a pep talk or a bit of encouragement was all that was needed, or all that I had to offer.

My son Rory, a recent graduate in Film & Drama from Trinity College Dublin, observed that a large number of people go out of business as a result of one simple, or final, act of greed, bad timing or over-reliance on bank borrowings. He had read many business books and had noted that many had been written by business journalists or university professors – very few were written by business entrepreneurs. So, with humour and ideas from Rory, we have scripted this simple set of observations. They will be invaluable in starting, adapting and managing most businesses.

I am a great fan of Ryanair, despite abhorring some of its mercenary practises, as it has provided many millions like me with a cheap, reliable mode of commuting around Europe. I can well recall the cost of air travel for the ordinary person prior to Ryanair's arrival. The 'National Airline' Aer Lingus, in partnership with British Airways, operated a duopoly on the Dublin/London route and screwed its captive audience. Eventually, British Midlands entered the market, despite strong resistance from the incumbents and subsequently, Ryanair arrived to create havoc for the established dinosaurs.

On one occasion whilst waiting at the airport, I purchased a book by Paul Kilduff, *The Little Book of Mick* – a book of quotations attributed to Michael O'Leary, the CEO of Ryanair. The quotes are hilarious but behind the bluster and expletives, the reader will observe an incredible no nonsense doctrine. It has resulted in Ryanair becoming Europe's most successful airline in the first decade of the new Millennium. With this in mind, you will forgive me for referring back to Ryanair on several occasions throughout this book.

Over the past few years, I have been bemused but not shocked by the revelations at Anglo Irish Bank plc and media publishers, INM plc. These companies were both perceived success stories on an international scale, managed by high profile personalities. Today, Anglo Irish Bank is remembered for deceit, greed, dishonesty and the lack of integrity displayed by some of its senior executives. In the case of INM plc, nepotism and incompetence contributed to its demise. Again, both organisations feature regularly in this book.

I have often browsed the book *Up the Organisation* by Peter Townsend, former CEO of Avis. Peter Townsend passed away on 29 August 2009, but his legacy is his book, with its crisp, common sense views on best business practice. I have relied heavily on the style and architecture of that book to guide me both in business and in writing this book.

During my research, I was introduced to a powerful book *Harmonic Wealth* by James Arthur Ray. I have been invigorated by his words of wisdom and analytical mind. Born in 1957, Ray is a motivational speaker and author and a *New York Times'* bestseller. However, in 2011, Ray was found guilty of negligent homicide, following the deaths of three participants in one of his motivational bootcamps.

Humour, jokes and quotes have come from a multitude of sources, including friends, too many to mention or indeed to remember. Cartoons are courtesy of Tom Halliday, Arnaldo Almeida and Dan Rosandich. The cover page is also courtesy of Tom Halliday.

For views and guidance, I contacted many local and internationally successful entrepreneurs. To the small number of business leaders who accepted my phone calls and gave generously of their time and experience, I am extremely grateful. To those that would neither accept nor return my calls......what can I say – I hope your customers have better luck.

Rory has been my enthusiastic co-author. I hope you enjoy the read and if you are up to it, say hello to Rory on Facebook. All comments and suggestions will be acknowledged.

Enjoy the read.

Gerry

CHAPTER 2
Adapting to change

Jimmy received a parrot for his birthday. The parrot was fully grown, with a very bad attitude and a worse vocabulary. Every other word it uttered was an expletive; those that weren't curses were, to say the least, rude.

Jimmy tried to change the bird's attitude, by constantly saying polite words, playing soft music – anything he could think of. Nothing worked. He yelled at the bird, and the bird got worse. He shook the parrot and the bird got madder and ruder.

Finally, in a moment of desperation, Jimmy put the parrot into the freezer. For a few moments, he heard the bird swearing, squawking, kicking and screaming. Then suddenly there was absolute silence. Jimmy was afraid that he might have actually hurt the parrot, and quickly opened the freezer door.

The parrot nervously stepped out onto Jimmy's extended arm and said: 'I'm sorry that I offended you with my language and my actions, and I ask your forgiveness. I will endeavour to change my behaviour.'

Jimmy was astounded at the change in the bird's attitude. He was about to ask what had changed him, when the parrot continued: 'May I ask what the chicken did?'

* * * *

As quoted above, Charles Darwin stated: 'It is neither the strongest of the species that survives, nor the most intelligent but the one that is most responsive to change.'

In the past 24-hours, 367,000 new human beings have been born and 172,000 people have died. The world is a dynamic place; nothing remains the same. Therefore in business, you must assume that change is taking

"I hope this diversification plan of yours has legs......"

place, every moment of the day; even if you cannot see it. As exemplified by the recent changes in the retail industry, the small corner shop that did not see the evolution of the supermarket and the market town that did not see the arrival of the out-of-town shopping centre have been commercially obliterated. Solid state MP3 players are rapidly replacing the CD. Travel agents are becoming extinct as a result of the Internet.

In 2008 there was a rapid deterioration in the value of Sterling against the Euro. Then, in 2009, there was a temporary reduction in the UK Valued Added Tax (VAT) rate to 15%. These two events posed immediate challenges for the Republic of Ireland's retail trade. Shoppers flocked to the northern side of the border, in their thousands. Eventually in December 2009 the Government of the Irish Republic responded with a half a percentage reduction in the VAT rate, bringing it to 21%. They also reduced the excise duties on alcohol by a nominal amount, in the hope that it would arrest the outflow of retail spend. It was a case of too little, too late.

A further, and increasing, challenge for the retail trade and the owners of retail investment properties is the growing usage of the Internet for online shopping. This will lead to retailers being unable to pay existing rents, as turnover falls or gross margins are slashed to compete with the online competition. It is inevitable that most retailers will have to adopt an online presence. Retailers can consider their premises as a window for their businesses, lending them a face and credibility with online shoppers.

Within the business community there are three types of person:

Firstly, there are those that are all the time looking for new ways to increase their business. They adapt to change as if on auto-pilot.

Secondly, there are those that do not like change. They feel threatened and fear for their future in the changed environment. Gradually they can be persuaded that change is on its way, with or without them. Eventually they adapt, accept and enjoy the change.

Thirdly, there are those that are blind to change. They refuse to recognise that it is already happening. They resist the most modest of changes. This is typical of many trade unions and ultimately their members become unemployed as enterprises go out of business or employers re-locate.

In your business, whether you are in the retail sector or not, it is essential to open up your mind to the changes that will surely come and challenge your existing business model.

* * * *

Jim was explaining to his friend that his wife had been cooking dinner and had gone out to the vegetable garden to cut a head of cabbage. When she did not return, he went outside, only to find that she had keeled over and died.

'What did you do then?' asked the friend.

'Ah,' replied Jim, 'I just had to open a can of peas.'

> **SUMMARY:** Always assume that change is happening, even if it's not immediately obvious, that will impact negatively on your business. Spend some time regularly investigating the changes in technology, in customer tastes, in the environment or in the business climate – anything that might affect your business.
>
> Be prepared and have planned your response.

CHAPTER 3
Advertising

'Advertising is the fine art of making you think you have longed for something all your life that you have never heard of before.'

Most advertising simply does not work. In general avoid it. It is mostly money down the drain. Occasionally, if you have a 'big message,' then it may be worth considering the best way to inform the public or target potential purchasers. For example, the Ryanair advertisement 'One Million Free Seats' was a promotion that was worthy of an advertising spend.

If you use an ad agency, fire it. From time to time you might need the creative assistance of an expert to design the ad copy. Find the one-man band, as opposed to fat cat agencies, where the first question asked is usually the size of your budget. Explain your objectives to your designer and the result you expect from the ad campaign. Ask him/her to return with a presentation, which you will either accept or reject. Follow the maxim: 'Don't own a dog and bark yourself.'

Consider the appropriate medium for your advert; newspapers, magazines, billboards, fliers, TV, radio or Internet. The distribution method for your message is by far the most expensive and critical aspect of any promotional campaign. Of the old mediums, radio has to be the best. Firstly, the listener receives the radio content free of charge, unlike in a newspaper. Secondly, the listener can be doing other activities, like driving home from work, while receiving your message at the same time. Thirdly, unlike newspaper ads, the listener cannot miss your message. If the radio is on, the message is being delivered. However, while radio adverts still serve a purpose, the world of communication has changed dramatically in the last decade. The old advertisement mediums are being overtaken, for efficiency and effectiveness, by cyber technology.

If you have some exceptional and unique quality product or service to promote, blogs on the internet are by far the cheapest and the most effective medium to use to get a reaction and they are virtually free. Facebook business (as opposed to Facebook social) is rapidly making an impact and will seriously erode the turnover of traditional advertising mediums.

In his book, *World Wide Rave*, David Meerman Scott highlights the approach of Cindy Gordon, Vice President of New Media Marketing at Universal Orlando Resort, when she launched the plans for the theme park, The Wizarding World of Harry Potter. Instead of spending million of dollars on Super Bowl TV ads, direct mail campaigns and magazine ads, she chose to tell just seven people. The seven were selected because they were rabid fans of Harry Potter.

These seven people told several thousand more fans via blogs. The mainstream media saw those blogs and wrote about the plans for the theme park in their newspaper and magazine articles, in TV and radio reports and in blog posts. As a result, it is estimated that some 350 million people around the world were informed of the plans to build the Harry Potter theme park.

'Pay per click' by Google is equally popular but can be pricey. If astutely managed, each and every day, by a competent, responsible staff member, it has the major advantage of establishing the conversion rate from 'click to sale'. Value for money expended can also be ascertained every single day.

Alternatively, the promotional budget can be used directly to benefit the customer. This worked in the instance of a new restaurant which was given a low-key, soft launch, with a small amount of money being expended on a local radio station promotion: 'Two meals for the price of one.' The actual product was also of the highest quality, served in the most ambient of settings. It was a huge and instant success.

The 'two for the price of one' offer was dropped after the first month of opening but the customer experience had been so good that business continued to grow through repeat and new business, with very favourable comments from patrons.

Equally, when you hear or see a restaurant continuously advertising 'run of the mill' messages, avoid it. If it was any good and offering value for money, you would have heard of it through a recommendation on the gourmet grapevine. When in foreign or unfamiliar territory, the best restaurants are those where you have to queue to get a seat. This will be where the locals and repeat visitors eat and these factors will have identified for you what advertising could never have achieved.

Over the years, continuous and relentless expenditure in the promotion of certain products and services has resulted in catch phrases becoming associated with these products, including:

'Beanz means Heinz!'

'Don't forget the fruit gums mum.'

'My Goodness, My Guinness.'

'Put a tiger in your tank.'

'No manager ever got fired for buying an IBM.'

'Kills all known germs.'

'It's good to talk.'

'It's finger lickin' good.'

'The mint with the hole.'

Despite all this recognition, young people now buy Apple computers and never purchase a packet of Polo mints; drivers put the cheapest fuel in their tanks, from the most conveniently located service stations; and Mum, on health grounds, doesn't buy sweets for the kids; most kids prefer a McDonalds' 'Happy Meal', with the free toy, to a Kentucky Fried Chicken bucket; talking on the phone is universally accessible due to mobile phones so you don't need BT either; own brand bleach is now the favourite, as it is usually 50% cheaper than Domestos; Guinness stout or porter with the white head is unlikely to be good for you; and beans from Heinz taste identical to the own label beans which can be purchased at a fraction of the cost.

> **SUMMARY:** For your business, the best advertisements are those from satisfied customers, who speak favourably of both your service and product.
>
> If you must advertise, limit it to delivering the big message.

CHAPTER 4
Ambience

The dictionary definition of ambience is: 'the atmosphere of a place.' This is an important element to get right for an enduring relationship between customer and supplier. Ambience is free of charge. It costs nothing to create a good atmosphere within an organisation. It is primarily driven by the attitude of the people that you meet, or speak with, in the course of your business. It is also a function of the surroundings. For example the appropriateness of the clean, clinical look of the dentist's surgery as opposed to the warm, cosy feel of the boutique hotel. A good ambience is essential within the hospitality industry, although it's also important in other business sectors.

My neighbour recently related the following story to me: 'Many years ago my wife and I frequented, for the first time, a nearby neighbourhood pub for a drink. On entering, we were immediately confronted, eyeball to eyeball, by a tall male with a large smile. His outstretched hand took that of my spouse and, with a hearty handshake, welcomed her to his establishment and introduced himself as Peter. I subsequently received the same treatment.

The premises were virtually full. We were shown to a table by the same gent and our drink order taken and promptly served. The buzz of conversation, the soft lighting, the comfortable chairs, the spotlessly clean glasses, the clinically clean washrooms and the friendly, efficient staff have ensured that for the past 27 years we frequent that same establishment regularly.'

Unfortunately, most businesses fail to recognise the need to create an ambience. Regularly staff that clearly dislike both their job and their customers, serve you – one might describe them as: 'having a face like thunder.'

On one occasion I had queued to be served for several minutes in a shop and eventually my turn came. As I was explaining my requirements, the staff member's mobile phone rang. The call was answered and after a few minutes, of what was clearly a personal conversation, noticing my agitation, the staff member moved behind a screen to continue the chat for a few more minutes, before returning to me. I received neither a word of apology nor explanation.

"He may be ready to see me now, but I'm not ready to see him......."

A positive ambience is free of charge but its implementation requires sound leadership qualities. The person in charge needs to encourage staff to contribute to creating the atmosphere required. If the CEO or proprietor is grumpy, arrogant, abrupt, rude, ill-tempered or bad mannered, this will be taken on board by the staff, who will dish this attitude out to the customers. Fly Ryanair and see for yourself.

In every city in the world, a street full of restaurants can be found, with two or three always packed and the rest relying on business from the overflow or from uninformed tourists or visitors to the area. The reason for this is usually straightforward – the successful establishment has created a combination of the best food, at the best value for money, not necessarily the cheapest, but in the most ambient of settings. The less successful restaurateurs speak of recession, fall-off in tourism, the bad weather, the hot weather or the deteriorating exchange rate, blah, blah, blah ....

SUMMARY: It is an increasingly competitive market in every type of business. You can obtain, free of charge, an advantage over your competitor. Look at your business and consider the relevance of ambience and where it is present or absent in your day-to-day operation and interaction with your customers. If it is missing, set a plan in motion to create it and then monitor the difference in your sales, customer satisfaction and in your profits.

CHAPTER 5
Auditors

The auditor from the Taxation Investigation Department was not surprised to see Grandpa show up with his solicitor.

The auditor said: 'Well sir, you have an extravagant lifestyle which the Tax Inspector finds hard to believe is funded solely from your gambling activities.'

'I am a successful gambler and I can prove it. How about a demonstration?' replied Grandpa. 'I'll bet you a €1,000 that I can bite one of my eyes.'

'OK, it's a bet,' said the auditor.

Grandpa removes his glass eye and bites it.

The auditor's jaw drops.

'Now, I'll bet you €2,000 that I can bite my other eye,' adds Grandpa.

The auditor can see that Grandpa is not blind so he accepts the bet.

Grandpa removes his dentures and bites his good eye.

The unfortunate auditor is growing alarmed, having bet and lost €3,000, with Grandpa's solicitor as a witness.

'Wish to go double or quits?' asked Grandpa. 'I'll bet you €6,000 that I can stand on one side of your desk and pee into that wastebasket on the other side, without getting a drop anywhere in between.'

The auditor, twice burned, is cautious now, but he looks carefully and decides there's no way this old guy could possibly manage that stunt, so he agrees again.

Grandpa stands beside the desk and unzips his pants, but although he strains mightily, he can't make the stream reach the wastebasket on the other side, so he pretty much urinates all over the auditor's desk.

The auditor leaps with joy, realising that he has just reversed the major loss.

But Grandpa's own solicitor moans and puts his head in his hands.

'Are you okay?' the auditor asked.

'Not really,' the solicitor said. 'This morning, when Grandpa told me he'd been summoned for an audit, he bet me €25,000 that he could come in here and pee all over your desk and that you'd be happy about it!'

* * * *

The overall duty of the auditor is to give an opinion on the truth and fairness of the financial accounts. There are many recent examples where the opinion of the auditor was at total variance with the facts. There has been case after case where companies reporting profits were in reality making astronomical losses.

Enron is a prime example. It was founded by a Kenneth Lay in 1985. By 1992, it was the largest trader of natural gas in North America. In an attempt to achieve further growth, Enron pursued a diversification strategy. By 2001, Enron had become a conglomerate that both owned and operated gas pipelines, pulp and paper plants, broadband assets, electricity plants, and water plants internationally. The corporation also traded in financial markets for the same types of products and services.

As a result, Enron's shares rose, from the start of the 1990s until year-end 1998, by 311%. The shares increased by 56% in 1999 and a further 87% in 2000. By December 2000, Enron's market capitalisation exceeded $60 billion, 70 times' earnings and 6 times' book value was an indication of the stock market's high expectations about its future prospects. In addition, *Fortune* magazine's 'Most Admired Companies' survey rated Enron as the most innovative large company in America.

Subsequently, it emerged that the financial results for Enron were massively overstated and that the company was, and had been for several years, loss making and insolvent but that this was concealed by the use of Special Purpose Vehicles, some of which were located abroad. Enron's auditor, Arthur Andersen, was accused of applying reckless standards in its audits because of a conflict of interest over the significant consulting fees Anderson earned from Enron. In 2000 alone, Arthur Andersen earned $25 million in audit fees and $27 million in consulting fees from Enron.

When news of the Securities and Exchange Commission (SEC) investigation of Enron was made public, Andersen attempted to cover up any negligence in its audit by shredding several tons of supporting documents and deleting nearly 30,000 e-mails and computer files.

> **SUMMARY:** The audit of your organisation should be seen as a welcome and useful service, performed by an independent third party. The auditor needs to be competent, energetic and interested in understanding your business. The organisation should benefit from the annual audit.
>
> As a rule, put the audit out to tender every 3 years; accept the lowest quote and exclude the Audit Firm from providing any other advice or services to the company during the period when it is auditor.

CHAPTER 6
Banks

'A banker is a fellow who lends you his umbrella when the sun is shining and wants is it back when it is raining.'

(Mark Twain)

One of life's disappointments is discovering that the man who writes the bank's ads is not the one who makes the loans.

A good and responsive banking system is a vital organ in the commercial life of a country. Without bank credit, the modern economy cannot grow and will gradually decline.

For the individual company or entrepreneur, a helpful bank manger is almost a prerequisite for commencing and growing a business. However, as is now the case, never assume that you have a friendly bank. A bank has no loyalty. If you find yourself in financial trouble and confide in your bank manager, do not be surprised if your account is quickly passed over to another executive and the terms and conditions of your loan and overdraft facilities are reviewed to your disadvantage.

Traditionally, the bank manager ranked in the local community as a person of great wisdom and commercial experience; he was seen as a person of integrity. Today, the public perception of bankers is very negative. Much of this has been fuelled by revelations about the personal greed, deviousness, deceit and inappropriate behaviour of several senior bankers. The local bank managers are now fundamentally administrators, with all their discretion removed and they have minimal authority. Banks, or rather the senior executives, are running for cover, having contributed significantly to putting the world economy into a recession. They are now only interested in self-preservation. Your past loyalty will count for zero.

SUMMARY: The moral of the story is not to put all your business into one bank. Spread the business around, possibly over three banks. It is better to have a track record with several banks and to have them vying for your business in times of good liquidity. In times of illiquidity and tight availability of credit, there are then at least options for you to explore between banks. It is a pointless exercise trying to start a new banking relationship in times of market turmoil in the financial sector.

CHAPTER 7
Bank Borrowings

Before you seek out bank finance for a project think very carefully about two key aspects. You must borrow more than enough to acquire or complete the project and secondly you must have a float in reserve, to ensure that you can meet the repayment instalments.

Taking the first point, it will be next to impossible to top-up your loan facility, by way of an extra amount, if you subsequently discover that you have underestimated your loan requirements. Requesting an extra top-up, halfway through a project, suggests to the bank that you got your figures wrong, which would be true, and that you are not as competent as you appeared when you were granted the original facility.

The solution is to initially try to borrow more than you need. This wriggle room will also be of use if the cash flow from the project falls short and is insufficient to service the repayment instalments in the beginning. Your float will also be useful to cover this shortfall.

Your loan application to the bank should not extend to more than one page. Good banking practise wishes to establish: who the borrower is; what their repayment ability is; and finally what is the security. The loan application should also set out the amount required, the purpose, the proposed repayment period, frequency of repayments and the interest rate structure that is acceptable to the applicant.

Send your loan application to the three banks where you are best known and await the replies.

Unless the loan is to purchase or refurbish the family home, do not offer personal guarantees, nor make your spouse a signature to the loan facility. If the loan facility is to be granted in your own name, specifically address the issue of the family home and clarify that it is not an asset that can be called upon to settle the liability. Have it inserted as a clause in the loan facility letter.

If it is a corporate loan and the bank is insistent on a personal guarantee, there are three critical aspects, which you must address. Again, insist that the family home is not part of any 'distressed' settlement and that the bank accepts that it falls outside the scope of any asset that may be 'grabbed,' in the event of default on loan repayment. Secondly insist that the personal guarantee is for a finite time, say three years, and thirdly ensure that your personal liability is capped at a figure, say 25% of the loan drawdown.

On the matter of the family home, it will be stressful if you are in default of a loan repayment and being pursued by the bank's collection department. Do not bring such misery onto your spouse and children by involving the family home. Needless to say, never agree to a second charge or mortgage being put on the family home.

> **SUMMARY:** Avoid any involvement by your spouse, that would put the family home at risk of being seized in settlement of a debt.
>
> Borrowing money carries risks. Do not be so over-confident that, prior to drawdown of the facility, you do not identify and quantify these risks and their possible impact on your business, yourself and your family.

CHAPTER 8
Barristers

Q. A barrister falls into shark-infested waters, but isn't attacked. Why?

A. Professional courtesy!

"Remember those legal reports on my public liability that you prepared?......."

In the legal systems of the UK, Ireland and other former outposts of British occupation and colonial rule, not only may you require the services of a solicitor but you will usually also have to employ a barrister. The barrister is briefed by the solicitor and is regularly an old school or college chum. The client may not engage or deal with the barrister directly. It's against the rules!

Check around before you sanction the use of a particular barrister, as legal outcomes are not necessarily the product of justice but can often depend on the adversarial and debating qualities of the barrister.

'An incompetent barrister can delay a trial for months. A competent barrister can delay a trial forever.'

If a legal opinion is required, ensure that it is being sought from a barrister that specialises in that particular field of law. Otherwise you are likely to end up with a lengthy, mumble-jumble of a document, with virtually equal but opposite outcomes of the dispute being advocated. Apart from a reduction in your bank balance, you will be none-the-wiser from learned counsel's opinion.

For a greater insight into the 'Barristing Profession' see the film *A Fish called Wanda*, starring John Cleese.

> **SUMMARY:** There are many fine and able barristers who work diligently and competently on behalf of their clients. It is the archaic system inherited from the British occupation that is inappropriate, inefficient and expensive for the client.

CHAPTER 9
Board of Directors

The Board is commonly made up of the Chairperson, Chief Executive Officer (CEO), senior employees and external appointees, the latter being referred to as Non-executive or Independent Directors. The latter group are in theory independent but, unfortunately, in most companies they are essentially appointees of the Chairperson or even the CEO. They are therefore usually neither effective nor independent.

"..and I think I can say, without fear of contradiction..."

Regularly you will find the same Non-executive Directors on several Boards; sort of a club for Directors. Being a Non-executive Director can be a nice little fee earner, recouped by attending four to six meetings per annum, per directorship, usually followed by a good lunch. This is most unhealthy, (not the good lunch) as there are many examples where the Board of Directors has failed to do the right thing due to blind loyalty to the CEO. In such appointments the Non-executive Director will resist asking any awkward questions so as not to 'rock the boat' or embarrass his/her friend the CEO. Equally, the Non-executives are regularly treated like mushrooms – kept in the dark and fed horse shit.

In one memorable case, involving the Irish and UK quoted company DCC plc, the Board supported the CEO Jim Flavin, even after the highest court in the land had concluded that he was guilty of wrong doing. One Irish Supreme Court judge referred to Flavin's activity as 'a fraud on the market'. This is a most serious offence, punishable by up to ten years in prison.

The Chairman of DCC plc was Michael Buckley, who, up to 2005, had been CEO of the publicly-quoted bank, AIB plc. This was the bank that required a multi-million pound taxpayers' bailout in 1985, after a failed diversification into an insurance company, ICI, threatened to bring the bank down. Subsequently, in 2000, AIB was discovered to be defrauding the Irish Revenue of many millions of pounds by withholding taxes on deposit interest, facilitating tax evasion and overcharging customers on foreign exchange transactions. In 2004, revelations emerged that AIB had been operating a tax evasion scheme, later known as the Faldor scandal, for its top executives that operated through the Virgin Islands. It also emerged that the bank's investment arm, AIIM, had been allocating profits to their favourite clients, to the disadvantage of other clients, again in the Virgin Islands. In 2008, AIB once more required a bailout of several billion Euro from the Irish taxpayer. Inevitably in 2010, it asked for, and received, a further multi-billion Euro cash injection from the Irish Government.

Apart from the fact that Buckley was employed by a bank that was incompetent and specialised in fraud and dishonesty, there is nothing to suggest that Buckley had a hand or knew of these illegal activities. Also, Buckley had not been a director of DCC plc when Jim Flavin had committed the crime of insider dealing. Another supporter of Flavin and a Non-executive Director of DCC plc was Maurice Keane, the former CEO of Bank of Ireland.

In the eyes of the public and wider investment community immense damage was done by the DCC Board supporting Flavin. The message being sent to other corporate executives was that the laws of the land did not apply, as long as the activity produced a profit.

"You don't have to worry about insider trading anymore...
we're firing you!"

SUMMARY: Unfortunately, the role which the directors should perform in the company, in theory, is rarely possible due to the incestuous nature of many Boards. The Independent or Non-executive directors should have a maximum period of service, limited to four years per company and they should be barred from serving on other Boards at the same time, where there are common cross directors. These limitations would assist in reducing the familiarity and 'Club' mentality that develops between 'Independent' Directors. It would also create opportunities for more people to serve as Non-executive Directors and would reduce their financial dependence on being re-elected.

CHAPTER 10
Bonuses

Bonuses are a common part of the remuneration package in many organisations, as a reward for achieving a financial target. They are paid out, on average, twice a year. In theory, a system of bonus awards is an incentive to the line managers and staff to obtain greater results. However, the bonus system that operates in many companies is dangerous and can lead to very serious medium to long-term difficulties for the company. In the period 1995 to 2008, the level of bonuses paid in the financial services sector has had dire consequences for the viability of many financial organisations, in particular banks in the latter half of 2007.

In 2009, Royal Bank of Scotland (RBS) and Northern Rock, both fully or partly nationalised banks, proposed to pay out bonus rewards estimated at £1.4 billon even though RBS, which was then 68% State-owned, was expected to post record losses, estimated at £28 billion, for the previous year. In February 2010, RBS announced 2009 losses of £3.6 billion which included bonus pay-outs to staff of £1.3 billion. Barclays, which announced it would take advantage of the taxpayer-backed Government guarantee, proposed to pay out about £2.3 billion in bonuses, in 2009.

In a hypothetical situation, paying a bonus to an employee who has placed the entire assets of an organisation on the 50/1 long shot winner in the Kentucky Derby or the Aintree Grand National seems insane. In the financial industry, however, bonuses, equating to almost 45% of the profits, have been paid out to successful risk-takers, who sometimes adopt a risk strategy akin to the punter on the racecourse.

SUMMARY: There is ample evidence that the system of paying bonuses has not been based on criteria that is beneficial to the shareholders. A better system of bonus remuneration is to allocate share options which cannot be sold for at least seven years after the date of granting. This will help to focus the employee on ensuring the medium to long-term stability, sustainability and profitability of the company.

CHAPTER 11
Brevity

This is important in all aspects of reporting and disseminating management information. The longer the spiel the less readable and less likely it is to be understood. Get down the important facts as quickly as possible and, if deemed necessary, append some further explanations for those that have the time and inclination to read them.

My colleague was once engaged by a tenant to negotiate a significant reduction in rent from the landlord. He was provided with a file of detailed weekly management accounts, in case they might be needed in the negotiations. The information file contained data on gross profit per product per week, employee hours per hourly rate, sales of each product and each division and more of the same. He was struck by the volume and level of detail provided and could only wonder at the cost and time spent producing such volumes of data, especially on a weekly basis.

He spent some time analysing the figures and summarising various bits of information to get the bigger picture. After several hours, he was surprised to discover that, even if the landlord reduced the rent to zero, the enterprise would still be making a loss. He reported this back to the Directors and they subsequently confirmed that his interpretation was correct. They were even more surprised. They had all received the information on a weekly basis for some 20 months and, apart from recognising that there was a weekly 'cash burn',' had not realised that the business model was an absolute flop and that it could never make a profit, irrespective of the level of rent. Within a year, the business had been liquidated.

> **SUMMARY:** In your business, identify the critical information that is needed on a regular cycle and which forms the basis for decision making. The information must be current, up-to-date, accurate and cheap to assemble.

CHAPTER 12
Budgets

'A budget tells us what we can't afford but it doesn't stop us buying it.'

(Anonymous)

The budget is a plan of income, expenditure and cash flow over a given period of time. Budgeting lies at the foundation of every financial plan. It's a resource to help you understand and measure the actual performance of your business, against your expectations and requirements. A budget can be very valuable if the time is taken to accurately dissect the arithmetic and the relationships between sales, cost of sales and your expenses, and to then integrate this into a cash flow.

It is fascinating to see the number of companies who produce an annual budget and its only use is to highlight variances between actual figures achieved and those figures in the budget on a monthly basis. In particular, where the variances are negative, the information should be used quickly to devise an action plan to get back to budget.

This rarely happens until cash flow requires some drastic steps, such as a rights issue, more bank debt or a redundancy and scaling back solution.

SUMMARY: Take the time to prepare the budget. It needs to be adjustable as throughout the period it covers unforeseen events can arise.

The negative variances between the budget and actual need to be highlighted on a timely basis and corrective action must be implemented, to bring the actual back on track. If this is not done, the budget simply becomes a waste of time.

CHAPTER 13
Bullying

Workplace bullying is endemic in many organisations, including the State sector, universities, army, media and the private sector in small and large corporations. In the schoolyard, bullying is usually a physical thing but in the corporate world, it raises it head in many shapes and formats – through exclusion, isolation, public reprimands, sarcastic remarks, name calling, ridicule, assignment of too much work or very little work, nit-picking and fault-finding.

'The effect on victims ranges, from poor physical health to mental stress, depression, insomnia and in some cases it can even lead to suicide. Bullying often results in a dysfunctional workplace, a high rate of stress, absenteeism, poor performance and resignations.'

(T. Byrne & K. Maguire, Irish Independent.)

Below is a brief summary of two of the ways of dealing with bullying:

The Informal: The victim needs to confront the bully in a calm atmosphere and explain that the behaviour is most unwelcome and is not acceptable. Most bullies are people of low personal esteem, who feel threatened, have a need to control others, have a poor self-image and are generally unhappy with their own lives.

When confronted in this manner, they will escalate the bullying or deny the issues. Denial is often their only response to being confronted. If necessary, bring a work colleague or trade union representative with you to the meeting. The key thing to bring to the bully's attention is that a continuation of their actions is going to have consequences and that you will not hesitate to move to a formal solution.

The Formal: This is the legal option and is to be avoided if at all possible. With the assistance of a lawyer or some other professional legal adviser, prepare and present a formal complaint to your immediate superior, unless that happens to be the bully, where you would then go one step further up the hierarchy.

Once you have commenced this process, be mentally strong and determined to see it all the way to a final conclusion.

SUMMARY: Bullying is rampant in all walks of life. In business, it creates a negative atmosphere and can ultimately lead to financial and/or legal sanctions being made against the employer, where swift and appropriate action is not taken to combat and eradicate workplace bullying. Once reported to an employer, there is a legal onus on them to deal with bullying in a professional and structured manner, so that the complainant is protected from further attack.

CHAPTER 14
Business Consultants

Consultants are people who borrow your watch to tell you the time. Former executives who find themselves fired and unemployable regularly re-invent themselves as business consultants. They are able to tell you: 'If I was you I would do this or that…'

It's easy to talk the talk, with buzzwords and catch phrases. It isn't the consultants' money that is being spent. If their recommendation totally backfires and costs you a packet of money or the loss of goodwill, it can be explained away in consultants' speck as 'a rapid shift in the market'.

"Keep the meter running. I'm going to the toilet…."

'Last week, we took some friends out to a new restaurant, and noticed that the waiter who took our order carried a spoon in his shirt pocket. It seemed a little strange. When the sommelier took our wine order, I noticed she also had a spoon in her pocket. Then I looked around and saw that all the staff had spoons in their pockets.

When the waiter came back to serve our soup, I asked: 'Why the spoon?'

'Well,' he explained, 'the restaurant's owners hired a consulting company to revamp all our processes. After several months of analysis, they concluded that the spoon is the most frequently dropped utensil. It represents a drop frequency of approximately 3 spoons per table, per hour. If our staff is better prepared, we can reduce the number of trips back to the kitchen and save 15 person-hours per shift.'

As luck would have it, I dropped my spoon and he was able to replace it with his spare.

'I'll get another spoon next time I go to the kitchen instead of making an extra trip to get it right now',' he said.

I was impressed. I also noticed that there was a string hanging out of the waiter's fly. Looking around, I noticed that all the waiters had the same string hanging from their flies. So before he walked off, I asked the waiter: 'Excuse me, but can you tell me why you have that string right there?'

'Oh, certainly!' Then he lowered his voice. 'Not everyone is so observant. That consulting firm I mentioned also found out that we can save time in the men's restroom. By tying this string to the tip of you know what, we can pull it out without touching it and eliminate the need to wash our hands, shortening the time spent in the restroom by 76.39%.'

'That's great, but how do you put it back?'

Well,' he whispered, 'I don't know about the others, but I use the spoon.'

SUMMARY: Hiring consultants is popular with politicians and lazy executives who can't be bothered to do a bit of research, with a bit of commitment, to implement new ideas. Even if it isn't broke, consultants will recommend that you fix it. Otherwise there would be no fee and no role for them. Only the incompetent will feel the need to bring in a business consultant.

CHAPTER 15
Business Expenses

'We should outlaw business class travel. We should pack them into economy class rather than have the fat and overpaid, flying around on flat beds, farting and burping after they have eaten and drunk their fine wines'

(Attributed to Michael O'Leary, CEO Ryanair,
from *The Little Book of Mick*, Paul Kilduff.)

For many people business expenses are a code for tax-free remuneration. The system is frequently abused, sometimes to the extent that it causes a public outcry. There was the 2009 debacle of British Members of Parliament fleecing the public purse for living expenses. The regime was so lax that some elected Members of Parliament (MPs), and at least one Lord, were still claiming refunds for mortgage repayments for second homes located in London, even though the actual loans had been paid off in full. By 2011, a former MP and a Lord were committed to prison for embezzlement.

The Sunday Telegraph reported that Mr Kemp, the MP for Houghton and Washington East, claimed for two DVD players for his one-bedroom flat in the space of a month. He was also reimbursed for the cost of 16 bed-sheets and claimed for two flat-screen televisions, bought just a year apart.

A former Labour whip was also said to have bought goods, including a freezer and fridge, near his north-east England constituency, despite the London flat being designated his second home. He also charged the taxpayer £105.75 for an engineer to attend to his washing machine which he could not work out how to operate.

The Irish *Sunday Independent* broke a story in early November 2008 after an investigation by its business editor, Senator Shane Ross, and fellow journalist Nick Webb. They had looked into the business expenses being claimed by the officials of the State Employment Agency, FÁS.

Subsequently, Roddy Molloy, Head of FÁS, foolishly or arrogantly, offered to discuss the issue on a TV chat show. He was asked about the FÁS official who, along with his wife, purchased business class tickets, costing €12,021, for a three-week round-the-world trip. They took in destinations as exotic as Tokyo, Honolulu and San Francisco before flying back to Dublin via Frankfurt. Molloy confirmed he had signed the expenses claim and that the official was at an event in Tokyo on official business associated with the World Skills competition and with the graduate programme which FÁS operates in Japan. He claimed that the official: 'at his own expense, spent some time on the return trip coming back through the US.'

Quizzed on the necessity of FÁS's Chairman, the trade union boss Peter McLoone, accompanying Molloy on a €7,300 per-person return business class flight to Orlando, Florida for a week-long stay, Molloy pointed out that the city, 'also happens to be very close to the NASA facility where the shuttle lands and takes off from.' He then alluded to the special relationship he claims his organisation has built up with NASA, over a number of years, a relationship which has led to Irish students being given opportunities to work and develop their research skills within NASA.

Asked about the FÁS executives who billed the Irish taxpayer for pay-per-view movies, ranging in price from $12 to $34 that they then watched in their US hotel rooms, Molloy compared the price of pay-per-view movies to 'chicken-feed', asking the presenter: 'What's $10 for a movie?'

Molloy had seriously underestimated the public outcry provoked by his responses in the TV interview and he was subsequently forced to resign from his position.

There is a simple rule of thumb to use to identify legitimate expenses. They are expenses that are incurred by the company that are: 'wholly and exclusively necessary to carry on the business.'

* * * *

A businessman walked into a New York City bank and asked for the loan officer. He said he was going to Europe on business for two weeks and needed to borrow $5,000 to cover his out-of-pocket, business expenses.

The loan officer said the bank would need some security for such a loan. The businessman then handed over the keys to a Rolls Royce that was parked on the street in front of the bank. Everything checked out and the loan officer accepted the car as collateral for the loan. An employee then drove the Rolls into the bank's underground garage and parked it there.

Two weeks later the businessman returned, repaid the $5,000 and the interest which came to $15.41.

The loan officer said: 'We do appreciate your business and this transaction has worked out very nicely, but we are a bit puzzled. While you were away we checked and found that you are a multi-millionaire. What puzzles us is why you would bother to borrow $5,000?'

The businessman replied: 'Where else in New York City can I park my car for two weeks for 15 bucks?'

> **SUMMARY:** Stealing is the only appropriate word to describe the actions of those that abuse the business expenses regime. Get back to basics.
>
> The Revenue definition is the baseline to judge expenses by – those wholly and exclusively necessary to carry on the business.

CHAPTER 16
Business Ideas

The book, when it is written, on guaranteed successful business ideas would surely be an instant bestseller. Time after time, the frustrated employee or wannabe entrepreneur laments that they would love to set up their own business if only they could come up with a good idea.

"It'll never get off the ground......I'm out....."

Below are the accounts of a few entrepreneurs who just went for it.

Many years ago, Kevin, a bored State employee, started to sell Christmas trees from the driveway of his modest suburban house.

Initially his neighbours looked on in amusement. In his first year he sold several hundred trees, over a pre-Christmas period of 20 days. Growers of the trees were only too happy to find new sales' outlets and supplied Kevin on a sale or return basis.

Within a few years, he was the single largest retailer of Christmas trees in that city, much to the annoyance of his neighbours, as the street was literally grid-locked with purchasers for 20 days before Christmas each year. Subsequently, Kevin resigned his position as a State employee. He still retails Christmas trees each December and spends the remainder of the year acquiring and managing an ever-increasing property portfolio.

* * * *

John was made redundant from his job as a sales executive to the catering and retail trades for a tea and coffee supplier. Initially, despair set in, and John spent several months doing part-time work between various employers. I had reason to call to his home one evening and was invited into the sun-room for a chat.

Every 10 seconds or so, I heard a constant 'click' sound from his nearby garage. On inquiring, he led me into it to have a look. He displayed a machine that was making tea bags.

John had managed to source an old tea bag making machine for the cost of its carriage to his garage. With his knowledge of the tea business and blending techniques, he was up and running making tea bags, exclusively for the catering industry.

Several months later, on another visit to John's house, a lighter, but much more frequent 'clicking' sound was coming from the garage. It transpired that the demand for John's tea was such that he'd needed to rapidly increase production and he had acquired a new state of the art tea bag making machine.

As the demand continued to grow, John re-located his business, by way of a merger, with a local coffee supplier, and successfully grew that business up to his retirement. He sold his business and is now happily living in Spain.

Rod had been an officer in the army and at the age of 40 decided the time to move on had arrived. He was a keen sportsman and physical fitness fan, so much so that he believed that the executives of the 'Corporate World' could benefit from a program of military-style fitness training.

Rod spent many months locating an outdoor area that could accommodate an obstacle and assault course. Within two years of his army retirement, he had opened his assault course for the unfit business executive.

Modest interest was shown and modest turnover achieved. It was only when a participant at one of the courses requested Rod to organise a day's training for his son and his school mates to celebrate his son's 12th birthday that the real demand for the assault course emerged. It was suitably adapted for young people, up to the age of 12 years old, and facilities were installed nearby for parents to relax and have a barbecue.

Its popularity rapidly grew and it became a major business. During the summer vacations, the assault course is constantly busy with young people who love the sense of danger and achievement.

* * * *

Jack was a very articulate maths' teacher in a secondary school. He was very popular with both parents and pupils because of his ability to teach maths and help pupils to get good grades in exams. Soon, word spread and parents who had pupils at other schools hired Jack to give their children private tuition or grinds. Within several years, Jack had established a highly profitable second level grind school, attracting thousand of pupils each year.

Jack only employed the most competent teachers, who had an excellent track record of exam success. The school has continued to grow and, subsequently, Jack opened the first private university in that country. The quality of the courses ensures that it continues to grow in international esteem.

There are multiple opportunities available if you want to start a business with minimal funds. Think of a product or service that you personally find difficult to get in your locality. Elicit views from neighbours and friends in that area, specifically asking about the lack of such a service or product. If your own view is constantly reinforced, then investigate deeper. If you conclude that there would be a demand, some basic arithmetic will establish if you can reasonably expect to make a profit. Again, if the feedback is positive, get on with it.

SUMMARY: There is nothing magical or secretive about identifying a profitable business idea. There is a constant demand for new or improved products and services. Latch on to one and get started. But remember it's better to know how much you might lose if the venture flops, as the majority do, and if such a loss will cripple you going forward in the future.

CHAPTER 17
Business Lunches

There is no such thing as a business lunch. Can you imagine the type of business decision that must wait until the attendees can harmonise their diaries to agree on the date and select the restaurant?

Genuine business meetings can be arranged over the phone, in a couple of minutes. The parties can meet up, address the serious business issues at hand and arrive at a conclusion much more efficiently in an office or meeting room setting than in a Michelin Star restaurant.

It beggars belief that any serious business can be discussed in a restaurant, or indeed in a private dining room, with people munching and chewing food and consuming alcohol.

* * * *

Sean and Lar met in a restaurant for a business lunch.

Sean said: 'I have a good deal for you, Lar. When I was in Dublin Zoo recently, I happened to pick up an elephant they didn't need any more. I could let you have it for £3,000.'

Lar sipped his gin and tonic and said: 'Sean, what am I going to do with an elephant? I live in a third floor flat. I barely have room for my furniture. I can't even squeeze in a card table. So you think I'm going to buy an elephant?' Sean replied: 'I could let you have three of them for two grand.'

'Aha,' said Lar, 'now you're talking!'

SUMMARY: Like business expenses, the business lunch is almost always an abuse of the expenses' regime. It is generally disallowed in tax law as a legitimate expense. A corporate blanket ban on such activity is the solution.

CHAPTER 18
Business Plans

If you are setting up a business from scratch, a business plan is to be recommended, but is by no means essential. If the printed document is more than a few pages, it is probably not relevant.

Never use an accountant to devise your business plan. Seldom do accountants produce a business plan on behalf of a client that demonstrates that the proposed business would be a flop. After all, how would they get a fee for producing such a negative piece of information?

If you can not do the business plan yourself you should not go into business but should remain as an employee. After all, what is the big secret? Sales income, less outlays, equals profits. If you are giving credit to your customers you need to make sure that you get at least the same credit from your suppliers, otherwise you will soon run out of money. It is called cash flow. You can do the forecast on the back of an envelope.

As the business grows, a simple rolling business plan will help you set out your business road map and, with a one-page MS Excel spreadsheet, you will be able to keep yourself informed of the required financial parameters you need to stay in business. However, the fundamentals never change: the venture must be profitable and must have a positive cash flow.

Any business plan with a simple upward adjustment to the total projected sales figure, a reduction in the projected overheads and an extra half dozen assumptions, can predict a roaring success. This may partly explain why over 80% of new business start-ups fail in the first three years.

In the early days, the new entrepreneur may be tempted to acquire the trappings of the established business – a large office suite on the right side of town and a spanking new Range Rover or some other gas-guzzling monster, for him/herself. You can take it as a near certainty that this attitude will ensure the venture will not make it to the third anniversary.

SUMMARY: Simplicity is the key to successful business plans. Ensure you have the product or service and the distribution to the customer at a price that generates a profit. In your business plan remember that the terms of business with customers and suppliers need to create a positive cash flow.

CHAPTER 19
Call Yourself Up

In many instances, the first contact that your potential, and indeed existing, customer has with your company is the phone. Try calling your company yourself when you are on holiday or abroad. Act as if you do not know the required extension and enquire as to the appropriate person to speak to, to deal with a particular issue.

Human beings have all but been eliminated in such a process and endless 'phone trees' are now the order of the day. In some cases, unless you know the extension or the particular department that you are seeking, you will be in a perpetual phone tree, until you finally hang up from despair. Presumably you will then seek to bring your business to a competitor.

Make another call; assume you do not know your company's phone number and call Directory Enquiries for assistance. You might well find that the actual company number is not listed or that you are given the fax or some other redundant number.

SUMMARY: It costs very little extra money to have incoming calls to your business answered correctly, politely and accurately. It is a simple task but you will not know if it needs improvement unless you anonymously and regularly call the number up yourself.

CHAPTER 20
Car Parks

The first and last point of physical contact for a visitor or customer to many business premises is usually the car park. Regularly, company car parks are dull, dirty and unkempt. At times the best and most convenient places are reserved for Directors and senior management. This is particularly noticeable in State and semi-State organisations.

"They sure know how to look after their customers!"

In many shopping centres, some areas of the multi-storey car park are continuously flooded, covered in chewing gum and serviced by minimal lighting. This immediately creates the wrong impression.

Think of the car park in the same way you would think of any other part of your premises that is open to the public. Smart décor, cleanliness and good lighting immediately give the impression of competent management and security, particularly for women.

SUMMARY: Abolish all reserved parking for Directors and staff. Reserve the best spaces for visitors and customers. The surplus spaces available to staff should be on a first come, first served basis. The staff member who seeks a parking space will make the extra effort to arrive early, in order to grab one of those unreserved spaces. Abolishing reserved employee spaces will also remove the sense of a hierarchy within the organisation.

CHAPTER 21
Cartels

'People of the same trade seldom meet together, even for merriment and diversion, but the conversation ends in a conspiracy against the public, or in some contrivance to raise prices.'

(Adam Smith, The Wealth of Nations, 1776)

A cartel is a formal agreement between firms where they agree to reduce competition, to the disadvantage of the consumer. It is ultimately about rigging the market in such a way that the firms involved all make more profit. Cartels regularly occur in industries where there are a small number of sellers and the product is usually homogenous.

The aim of the cartel is simply to increase profits for the members by rigging the price, depressing the total output for the industry, agreeing market share between members, allocating geographical locations between members and implementing other non-competitive devises and strategies.

In most countries, cartels are illegal. Below, however, are examples of some active cartels.

- OPEC: the organisation of oil producing States exists to control the cost of crude oil by restricting the level of oil production.

- Many trade organisations, especially in industries dominated by a few major companies, have been accused of being fronts for cartels.

- Labour unions are cartels, as they seek to raise the wage rates for labour by preventing competition.

In 2008, British Airways and Virgin Atlantic agreed to pay \$200m to settle a US class-action lawsuit to compensate eight million passengers who were the victims of an illegal fuel surcharge cartel.

For British Airways (BA) the penalty came on top of a £270m fine that had been levied by UK and US regulators the previous year, because of the airline's part in the fuel surcharge price-fixing scandal. Virgin Atlantic escaped the fine from the regulator as it blew the whistle on the cartel.

Including the above settlement, the case has now cost the airline around £338m. BA has yet to answer allegations brought by the European Union over the price-fixing of cargo fuel surcharges. There is still the possibility that senior BA staff could face criminal prosecution by the UK's Office of Fair Trading.

SUMMARY: Cartels are about cheating your customer, through overcharging them. It may be a criminal offence. Do not be tempted. If you are in an industry that could lend itself to a cartel arrangement, be careful how you tread – eventually you are likely to be invited into some anti-competitive practise that could ultimately be deemed a cartel. If you accept, you could find yourself facing criminal charges.

CHAPTER 22
CEO – The Role

'Any Chief Executive who doesn't have a sense of their own immortality is heading for disaster. They read articles describing themselves as visionaries and geniuses. They shouldn't believe it any more than when the press are calling them gobshites and wankers.'

(From The Little Book of Mick by Paul Kilduff.)

The CEO is the appointee of the Board. S/he is normally a Director and their role is to enhance the financial wealth of the shareholders. S/he will lead the company's management team, implement the strategic decisions of the Board and increase shareholders' financial wealth. The inspired CEO will seek, and be able to identify, the right person for the right role at senior management level within the organisation, ensuring that there are no round pegs in square holes and vice versa.

It is fundamental that the CEO should employ personnel who are more proficient than him/herself for the various roles within the organisation that report directly to him/her. Likewise, this philosophy needs to be repeated by the senior management team, in relation to those that report to it.

The inclusion of the CEO as a Board Member is not ideal. It is particularly difficult and awkward for the Board to discuss the performance of the CEO if s/he is present. There needs to be an appointed time slot, preferably at the end of the CEO's and Financial Director's presentation of the performance of the company since the last Board Meeting, where the CEO and other Executive Directors abstain themselves. This provides an opportunity for the Independent Directors to have a more frank and open discussion about the performances of the CEO and Executive Directors.

* * * *

A young executive is leaving the office late one evening when he finds the CEO standing in front of the shredder, with a piece of paper in his hand.

'Listen,' says the CEO, 'this is a very sensitive and important document here, and my secretary has gone for the night. Can you make this thing work?'

'Certainly,' says the young executive. He turns the machine on, puts the paper in and hits the start button.

'Thanks',' says the CEO, as his paper disappears inside the machine. 'I just need one extra copy.'

SUMMARY: Good leadership qualities make a good CEO. Humility and honesty are also necessary traits. The ability to focus on the important company objectives and to not be easily distracted is also essential.

CHAPTER 23
CEO's Remuneration

The neck of some of the CEOs over the past two decades is mind-boggling. Remuneration packages in the millions: a seven, or even an eight, digit basic salary, a proportionate pension contribution to a defined benefit scheme, company plane, company car, expense account, share options, loans and a bonus.

As the recession started to take its toll, it became obvious that the job the stakeholders had believed was being done by these CEOs was very different from the job they were doing in reality. Company after company folded as a result of poor management, poor decisions and often outright deception by the CEO.

Anglo Irish Bank plc, the fastest growing bank in Europe is a case in point. The Chairman, Sean Fitzpatrick, formerly the CEO, and his appointees, fleeced the company, using over-generous pay packages, loans and benefits spanning the previous decade. When the 'shit hit the fan' it quickly became apparent that these remuneration packages were totally unjustified. Many thousands of shareholders lost their entire investment.

In one case, one of Fitzpatrick's divisional operating officers was given a €3.75m departure cheque, for services to the company. Ironically, within a few months, it came to light that the company was totally insolvent and has required a multi-billion State bailout. That same former executive is currently being sued by the bank, as it tries to re-coup from him a multi-million Euro loan.

In another case, Sir Freddie Goodwin, the departing CEO of the Royal Bank of Scotland, another insolvent bank that required a multi-billion pound bailout by the UK Government, was rewarded with a multi-million pound pension. It was way above his statutory and contractual entitlements.

SUMMARY: It is patently clear that a culture of absolute greed has been a dominant factor in the remuneration of many CEOs since the start of the new Millennium. Shareholders have been hoodwinked by distortion, deceit and legal larceny, perpetrated by remuneration committees in many companies.

CHAPTER 24
Charitable Donations

Most charities do good and useful work. It might confuse you at times to understand why the charity supporting Third World poverty operates from a plush office suite, in the upmarket area of town. Or that the CEO has a remuneration package commensurate with senior bank executives.

However, it is not the role of the corporation to make donations. It is wrong that stakeholders, collectively or individually, may not give a curse about a particular charity, yet they still have to witness their money being channelled in that direction.

"This is no way to be sure of collecting our dividends!"

Charity is an individual's personal response to a particular cause or need. It is difficult to fathom the mindset of the CEO or Board of Directors that would seek to spend stakeholders' funds on a particular charity.

The Non-Executive Directors who bring such requests to the Board or the CEO are the most useless and incompetent. Given the incestuous composition of these Boards, however, no-one has the courage to bin the suggestion.

* * * *

A blonde decided that she was tired of her empty soul-less life. She cut her hair, dyed it brown and set off for a drive. She wanted to do charitable acts of kindness to see if it would enhance her life.

While driving through the countryside, she came across a farmer who was trying to get his sheep across the road. She stopped her car and waved the farmer across, thinking this would be her first charitable deed.

After the sheep had all crossed, the blonde said to the farmer: 'Your sheep are so cute. If I guess how many there are, could I have one?'

The farmer thought it impossible and told the blonde it was a deal.

The blond replied: '637.'

The farmer was amazed that the blonde had guessed the exact number, but lived up to his bargain.

'I'll take that feisty one over there,' said the blonde.

Then the farmer said to the blonde: 'Okay, now if I guess the real colour of your hair, can I have my dog back'?

SUMMARY: Social responsibility is a modern catchphrase to explain the reasons why there are now corporate charitable donations. It is more equitable for the individual shareholders to make such donations from the dividends they receive, rather than for the corporation to engage in such activity.

CHAPTER 25
Chartered Accountants

Two accountants are in a bank, when armed robbers burst in. While several of the robbers take the money from the bank tellers, others line the customers up against a wall, including the accountants, and proceed to take their wallets, watches and so on. While this is going on, accountant number one jams something in accountant number two's hand.

Without looking down, accountant number two whispers: 'What is this?'

Accountant number one replies: 'It's that €50 I owe you.'

* * * *

In the corporate world, accountants start life as the bean counters. The bright ones usually progress rapidly up the ladder. They have generally led a protected life, by generating fees for doing the simple sums and accounting tasks that entrepreneurs simply can't be bothered to do.

Accountants are experts in telling the entrepreneur what s/he cannot or should not do. They are not entrepreneurs and they have little understanding of the role of sales personnel. It is therefore surprising that many of them make it to the most senior posts of very large industrial and financial enterprises.

'How can you tell when the Chief Accountant is getting soft?'
'When he actually listens to Marketing before saying: "No."'

By virtue of the access they have to the financial information within the company, they can often punch above their weight in the eyes of the less informed. They can usually talk the talk.

Within the accountancy profession, there is the 'Secret Society of Back Scratchers'. Not to be confused with, nor on a par with, P2 or the Freemasons, who are perceived to indulge in all types of wizardry and rituals. The 'Society of Back Scratchers' is in every nook and cranny of the business community of western enterprise. They look after each other and are to be found on committees, societies, advisory panels and in the top positions in industry and financial services.

Members advise Governments on aspects of taxation, annual budgets, capital spending, social policies, criminal law, electioneering and going to war. They are experts in everything. They are amongst the top earners in western economies.

An accountant was accosted in the street by a tramp begging for money.

'Spare some change, sir,' said the tramp.

'Why?' replied the accountant.

'Because I haven't a cent to my name and I haven't had a hot meal in three months.'

'Hmm,' said the accountant. 'And how does this compare to your previous quarter?'

SUMMARY: If you are employing an in-house accountant to do the routine management accounts, annual financial accounts and to manage the financial function, avoid those graduates of the large, international companies that arrive in the pin-striped suit, polished to a tee and can speak the buzz words. They will not know a debit from a credit but, once employed, will rapidly hire an assistant who will know how to produce meaningful management information on a timely basis. It is better to employ an accountant that actually knows how to perform the basic accounting functions. He is more likely a graduate from a smaller to medium-sized practice.

CHAPTER 26
Chauffeurs and Drivers

When the CEO believes that s/he needs the continuous services of a chauffeur or driver it highlights one of several things. The CEO has:

- Lost their driving permit due to alcohol abuse or drug abuse.
- Become physically impaired and is unable to drive.
- Is allergic to the smell of gasoline and cannot refill the fuel tank.
- Been influenced by old gangster movies where the boss or Don always has a driver.
- Their head up their *** and feels so important that s/he is above driving just in the same way that s/he wouldn't nip down to the store to fetch a carton of milk.

"May I introduce my sat nav......?"

Also, the chauffeur is handy to collect the kids from school, collect the spouse's laundry, put out the domestic garbage bins and even give the lawn a bit of a mow; all of course on the company payroll. What an abuse! The CEO has surely lost the plot and the Board needs to move swiftly into 'firing CEO mode'.

The prestige of having a chauffeur is particularly prevalent in political circles. There, the most junior government ministers, in the most bankrupted nations, beaver to get their butts into the black, chauffeur-driven Maria. It is a throw back to the Mafia – the chauffeur driven black limousine is the ultimate symbol that you are one of the 'bosses'.

* * * *

George Bush and his chauffeur accidentally hit and killed a farmer's pig while driving through the country.

Bush tells the chauffeur to apologise to the farmer. They drive up to the farm and the chauffeur goes inside.

He is gone for a long time. When the driver returns, he explains his long absence.

'Well, first the farmer shook my hand, then he offered me a beer, then his wife made me some cookies, and his daughter showered me with kisses.'

'Why were they so grateful?' Bush asks.

The chauffeur replies, 'I don't know. All I told him was that I was George Bush's driver and I'd just killed the pig.'

> **SUMMARY:** The need for a full-time chauffeur is a dangerous sign of arrogance and indicates that the CEO has lost touch with reality. This is unhealthy for the company – sooner or later a heavy price will be paid by the shareholders for tolerating such extravagances.

CHAPTER 27
Company Planes

During the technology and dot.com boom of the 1990s, paper multi-millionaire shareholding staff spent relentless hours becoming experts on private jets, just like those poorer young city traders had become experts on the latest Porsche or Lamborghini. Ownership of a private jet was the ultimate status symbol during this period. The majority of private jet owners had lost touch with reality.

"Dad, can I use the company airplane tonight?"

This was best demonstrated in 2008 when the CEOs of the insolvent, USA motor manufacturers, travelled to Washington DC. They were seeking billions of Federal Dollars to bail out the companies for which they had received multi-million dollar annual pay cheques to manage. When it came to light that each of the CEOs had travelled in their separate, corporate jets to plead for a handout, American public opinion quickly became less than sympathetic.

* * * *

One day Dick Cheney, George Bush and Laura Bush were in the presidential private jet, travelling over Europe.

George Bush said: 'If I throw out a €100 dollar bill, I will make somebody happy down below.'

Dick Cheney interrupted: 'If I throw out ten, $10 bills, I'll make ten people happy.'

Laura Bush interjects: 'If I throw out a hundred $1 bills, I'll make 100 people happy.'

The pilot thinks to himself: 'If I throw these three gobshites out of this jet, I'll make six billion people happy.'

SUMMARY: The ultimate status symbol is the corporate jet. The beneficiaries will usually have lost touch with reality. It could be a case of the company serving the needs of the executives rather than the other way around.

If you are a shareholder in a company that owns or regularly hires a corporate jet, assess the grandiose attitude of the executives and decide if you are getting a corporate commitment from them. If not, sell.

CHAPTER 28
Company Social Events

Typically the summer or Christmas party is an occasion for everyone within the organisation to let their hair down, in the relaxed atmosphere of the local hotel – usually without their life partners or spouses: A time for comradeship.

"Wiggins.....once a year, I enjoy coming down to your level..."

The CEO and one or two of the Directors and senior management might attend and because they are very busy, will arrive late. Anyhow, this group usually collectively squirms away into a corner on their own, to avoid contamination from the masses in the early part of the event. Later they emerge, after a tank-full of booze, to 'hit it off' with the secretaries and younger members of staff.

SUMMARY: The more progressive companies will have a culture where Directors, the CEO and senior managers will make a point of inviting all life partners and spouses of the staff, including their own and be the first to arrive at the event to welcome individually, each and every staff member and partner. They will seat themselves at various tables throughout the gathering and control their intake of alcohol.

CHAPTER 29
Conventions

Trade and association conventions are usually code for tax-free junkets and all-expenses paid holidays. Attending conventions and fact-finding missions are a favourite pastime of politicians and public employees. It is also a mechanism for repaying favourites, paying commissions and other financial kickbacks.

In 2009, eight Irish parliamentarians, with four State officials, attended a conference, the Inter-Parliamentary Union in Cape Town, South Africa, at a cost of €86,000. The Speaker of the Dáil (Irish Parliament), Ceann Comhairle John O'Donoghue, led the party. Subsequently, he was forced to resign, as opposition mounted against his lavish expenses.

In the corporate world, junkets are often arranged by suppliers of capital items like computer hardware, computer software or by medical drug companies who rely on the medical profession to prescribe their treatments. Behind this so-called 'transfer of product knowledge' it is well recognised that this type of generosity creates a loyalty in the recipients to the donors' brand. One might be forgiven for concluding that it is blatant bribery and verging on the corrupt.

It is bad enough that the executive or employee accepts such gifts but to compound the crime by placing an order for that product is a step too far. Where extravagant incentives are being used, to encourage or gain support or recommendation for a product or service, it must always be remembered that there is no such thing as a free meal.

* * * *

Sean and a friend stayed at a Chicago hotel while attending a bankers' convention. Since they weren't used to the big city, they were overly concerned about security. The first night they placed a chair against the door and stacked their luggage on it. To complete the barricade, they put the rubbish bin on top. If an intruder tried to break in, they would be sure to hear him.

Around 1 a.m. there was a knock on the door.

'Who is it?' Sean called out nervously.

'Honey,' a woman on the other side yelled, 'you left your key in the door.'

At one of the USA Democratic Conventions, Trojan Condoms had set up a pavilion where they handed out thousands of free condoms, apparently in case Bill Clinton turned up.

SUMMARY: There are conventions and conferences for every conceivable topic. The majority of these events are either junkets or holidays. There is little to be learnt from them. Many of the attendees never bother to attend the lectures or presentations but indulge in all the other social activities that go hand-in-hand with such proceedings. Where the 'public purse' is paying for their attendance, you will regularly see the spouses, partners and colleagues, all joining the party. This is a total abuse and, in some instances, is tantamount to theft.

CHAPTER 30
Contacts

A very important ingredient in business is to have contacts in all facets of life. It is an investment of your time to get to know, amongst others, the chief planning officer, the head of the local police, the main movers in the political establishment and the senior members of the press.

There are many ways to make contacts. The simplest is to lift your telephone, call direct and introduce yourself. A small number of the recipients will neither take your call nor call you back. They are generally the ones who are arrogant and full of their own importance.

Those who do take your call will be happy to have been introduced.

"Miss Gibbs.. stick a pin in 'Who's Who' and get them on the phone"

SUMMARY: Contacts are primarily useful for obtaining information and further introductions. Never put a contact in a position whereby your request puts him/her in a position where it would be unethical or a breach of duty for them to answer it. Never abuse the friendship. Good contacts are a lifetime's resource and need to be treated with respect.

CHAPTER 31
Corruption

Corruption is to be open to bribery or to be morally depraved. It is assisting others to steal, usually for financial gain. It is part of daily life in most African governments and to a lesser extent in Western governments. Corruption has brought down governments and nations and the largest corporations in the world. It is prevalent in the armament industries and regularly has the tacit support of world government.

In 2007, the UK Government confirmed that the UK arms' manufacturer, BAE, was being investigated for a series of corruption allegations relating to its activities in six countries. In essence the claims were that BAE paid bribes to members of National governments in order to win lucrative arms' contracts.

When the Serious Fraud Office controversially dropped a probe into a BAE arms' deal with Saudi Arabia, citing national security, it was assumed that the British Government had authorised the decision. The reality was that the Government did not wish to embarrass members of the Saudi elite who had sought financial kickbacks, prior to awarding contracts to BAE.

The Serious Fraud Office was also looking at claims regarding BAE in South Africa, Tanzania, Romania, Chile, the Czech Republic and Qatar. In addition to the corruption claims, they were also investigating allegations of bribery and fraud in Bosnia, Nigeria, Zambia, Costa Rica and Egypt. Insisting that no company was 'above the law' the British Government stressed that it would 're-double' its efforts to tackle corruption.

Many of these investigations have subsequently been abandoned which has undermined the UK Parliament, the rule of law and Britain's reputation for implementing anti-bribery legislation.

Kenneth Lee 'Ken' Lay (1942 – 2006) was an American businessman, best known for his role in the widely reported corruption scandal that led to the downfall of Enron Corporation, the largest trader of natural gas and other products in North America.

When the scandal broke in 2001, Lay and Enron became synonymous with corporate abuse and accounting fraud. Lay was the CEO and Chairman of Enron from 1985, until his resignation in January 2003.

Lay was found guilty in May 2006, on 10 counts against him, covering corruption and fraud. He faced up to 30 years in prison. Lay, however, died of a heart attack while on vacation in Colorado in July 2006, prior to a sentence being handed down.

SUMMARY: Corruption can certainly bring immediate financial gains to those prepared to perpetrate it. Such gains, however, can ultimately lead to investigations that absorb years of your life. Even if allegations of corruption cannot be proven, the very accusation itself can stick to you for the rest of your life.

CHAPTER 32
Customer Service

Every company claims high levels of customer service. The reality is that, the vast majority provide mediocre customer service. In many instances, 'Customer charters', 'customer mission statements' and 'customer is king' catch-phrases are common currency, with no substance behind them.

Real customer service cannot happen by chance, but requires continuous grooming and hard work. In his book, *Crowning the Customer* Feargal Quinn, believed that every business should be customer-driven:

'By customer-driven, I mean a company, where all of the key decisions are based on the over-ridding wish to serve customers better: A company, where everyone in it, sees serving the customer as their only business.... You need to be able to wear the customer's hat, to walk in their shoes.'

A customer service call centre, located in downtown Mumbai, India, may be the ideal choice if you are the accountant. However, for customers it is far from satisfactory if, for example, you are in Glasgow and cannot get your computer to work and you are being talked through a complicated re-boot process from half way around the world, by a heavily-accented Indian via a crackling phone line.

With Ryanair, the concept of customer service is somewhat akin to a blunt instrument strategy:

> *'Our customer service is the lowest prices guaranteed, on brand new aircraft, flying safely, on time, with the least risk of cancellation or a lost bag. Did you get that service? Yes, you did? Fine: Shut up and go away.'*

(Attributed to Michael O'Leary, CEO Ryanair)

77

SUMMARY: Despite greater awareness of the need for genuine customer service, it is sadly lacking in most organisations. The quality of service is best tested when schedules or events do not happen as planned and the customer needs assistance.

There is an initial cost involved in providing proper customer service but go the extra mile. You will reap the dividends for years to come, with repeat business from satisfied customers.

CHAPTER 33
Decision-Making

'I always look for a woman who has a tattoo. I see a woman with a tattoo, and I'm thinking, okay, here's a gal who's capable of making a decision she'll regret in the future.'

Decision-making can be regarded as an outcome of mental processes, leading to the selection of a course of action among several alternatives. Every decision-making process produces a final choice. The output can be an action or an opinion of choice.

'It is our choices... that show what we truly are, far more than our abilities.'

(Harry Potter and the Chamber of Secrets, J. K. Rowling, 1999.)

Within a business organisation many layers of decisions need to be made in the course of a year. Some of these are strategic and require thorough research before being implemented. They are a function of the CEO and the Board of Directors.

If the CEO has achieved his/her goal of employing subordinates that are better at their task than s/he would be, then day-to- day decisions, within agreed budgetary limits, are better left to line managers and division heads. But if the CEO insists on 'micro-managing' s/he could bring the organisation to a grinding halt: for example the Head of Cleaning needs the sanction of the CEO to change the brand of hand-wash liquid for the washrooms. It could take a week to reach such a decision when, in reality, it should only take a few seconds.

One day, after a man had his annual physical, the doctor came out and said: 'You had a great check-up. Is there anything that you'd like to talk about or ask me?'

'Well,' he said, 'I was thinking about getting a vasectomy.'

'That's a pretty big decision. Have you talked it over with your family?'

'Yeah and they're in favour 15 to 2.'

SUMMARY: Most decisions within an organisation are such, that to get some of them wrong will have no material impact on the performance of the company. The lack of a structure, whereby line managers and supervisors can make decisions, will be detrimental to an organisation. In this set-up the CEO will be party to each and every decision and will risk neglecting the key issues that create sustainable, shareholder wealth.

CHAPTER 34
Diversification

The history of business failures is littered with examples of profitable enterprises going bankrupt after diversification.

"He was a big cheese until he bought in to chalk......"

If the enterprise is cash rich, the first option to consider is returning the cash pile to the shareholders – not to spend it on their behalf, by investing in some half-baked idea like diversification.

When you see a fruit importer and distributor diversify into property investment, the recommendation is to view your shareholding as a 'sell'.

Having said that, there are cases where diversification can be rewarding. This is usually only where there is a strategic or supply chain link to the new business. For example, there may be some logic in the car fuel importer acquiring a chain of filling stations, to secure a retail presence. Also, the sandwich-maker may decide to acquire a bread-making factory.

Diversification of this type is usually better achieved by organic diversification as opposed to acquisition: at least the 'toe in the water' risk is much less, than the risk associated with the outright purchase of an existing business.

The history of Ryanair, over the period since the appointment of Michael O'Leary as CEO, has been one of an extreme dogma of organic growth by keeping the cost of air fares low. Over a period of 20 years, from starting out with a humble fleet of one turbo-prop aircraft, it is now Europe's largest carrier, with the modern fleet of 250 Boeing 737 Jets. Save for the purchase of Buzz, for €15m in 2004, and the purchase of 29% of the Irish 'National' airline, Aer Lingus, the solitary focus on driving down costs, and subsequently airfares, is the best example of organic growth in Europe, in recent times.

Instead of a clear focus on building up its core air travel business, Aer Lingus on the other hand lost its way and money on diversification. During its history, Aer Lingus had indulged in various growth strategies, like ownership of travel & holiday companies, hotels and even a computerised payroll company, Cara Pay.

SUMMARY: Do not be tempted to take your focus off your primary business, in the belief that easy profits can be made by diversification. It can appear that the neighbour's chicken is always fatter.

The core business will require continuous monitoring and the organisation will need to have the ability to change to consumer demands and other challenges. Diversification can be a negative, as it can be a distraction for the management.

CHAPTER 35
Employment Contracts

In so far as they go beyond the details that may be statutorily required, employment contracts have a habit of protecting the lazy and incompetent, to the detriment of the company.

Good and able executives do not need to be handcuffed to the company or protected by financial parachutes, in the event that it is merged or sold. Meeting the daily challenge, with success recognised and rewarded, is the only real criteria for motivating and maintaining executives' loyalty to the company.

SUMMARY: If the company is well managed, it is unlikely that the able, energised and progressive executive will be focused on switching allegiance to another company. Reward effort and results, instead of engaging in contractual loyalties.

CHAPTER 36
Excellence

The pursuit of excellence, in all aspects of a company's affairs, is a lofty goal that is generally not achieved. The first requirement is to be able to define excellence and to acknowledge that short-term profits go hand-in- hand with un-sustainability. This is often seen in the property development world where tomorrow does not matter, so long as there is a profit for today. Poor design, poor finishes, scant regard for the environmental impact, poor worker health and safety, are commonly witnessed in that industry.

In manufacturing there are the giants who strive for excellence and amongst the shining examples stood the Toyota Motor Corporation. Toyota had a long history of a quality product, with quality back-up service, delivered by a content and fulfilled workforce. In January 2010, the reputation of Toyota was severally tarnished, however, when in excess of 8 million vehicles had to be recalled for safety checks.

The typical property developer has a helicopter, a private jet, likes to attend horse racing and is paranoid about his need to have influence with politicians. He tends to dine in the best restaurants and can be found in the latest trendy night-clubs. The CEO of Toyota, Akio Toyoda, grandson of the founder, dresses in the company's standard industrial clothes, safety shoes and hard hat, and is virtually indistinguishable from the thousands of shop floor personnel. He eats in the same staff dining area and fetches his own coffee. When using air travel, he goes in steerage, unless on a long haul flight when he will choose business class. He clocks up some 2,600 working hours per annum, which is on a par with the typical Japanese industrial worker. His basic salary, however, is approximately three times the average industrial wage of his colleagues. Akio Toyoda is motivated by the challenge of excellence and long-term sustainable profitability for the shareholders and his co-workers. He believes in the philosophy of consensus management, continuous production improvements and in-depth investigation and analysis, before any strategic changes. No permanent staff members have been made redundant in the Toyota Corporation since 1937. The effects of the 2010 safety re-call have put thousands of jobs at risk. Greater productivity and cutting costs have reduced the reliability of Toyota cars.

"Dammit man!....Stand up straight when you're grovelling to me!.."

In Ireland, the former CEO of the public-quoted Anglo Irish Bank, Sean Fitzpatrick had an annual remuneration in excess of some 40 times that of the average employee in the bank. His portrayal as a 'superstar banker' and 'poster-boy banker' came to an abrupt end when his deceit and greed surfaced in December 2008. Subsequently the bank was nationalised at an estimated cost of €35 billion to the Irish taxpayer. All the shareholders lost the entirety of their investment which included many members of the bank's own staff, who were Sean's former colleagues. A criminal investigation into his activities is under way.

SUMMARY: Striving for excellence in your business organisation is not achievable if the CEO craves star status, is busy giving press interviews and is on the lecturing circuit. Inevitably s/he will become arrogant and the focus on excellence will be adjusted to promoting his/her own 'excellence'. The enterprise will soon lose its way.

CHAPTER 37
Far Away Fields are Green

The New Yorker can never make a profit in Texas. The Londoner cannot make a profit in Dublin and no foreigner can make a profit in France. Admittedly this is like saying: 'There are no pianos in Japan.' The point is, however, that if you cannot make a profit on your own doorstep, it is unlikely that you can make it further away from your home base.

Knowing your market is critical. It is difficult enough to identify and gauge the business opportunity in your own locality, as within it there are trading regulations and standards, employment legislation, taxation and statutory reporting requirements. These all present challenges for the entrepreneur.

In the early days of an enterprise, intensive hands-on management by the proprietor will be required. The effectiveness of this input is immediately diluted the further the enterprise is located from your local area of knowledge.

This can also apply to an individual's investment strategy. A colleague who is a significant star in the world of entertainment, would often over-ride his investment adviser's suggestions. He had a simple rule. He must be able to drive within an hour from his home and visit property or business ventures where he was an investor. Whilst the recession has knocked a hole in the earlier values attributable to these investments, he is still well ahead of his original cost. He had a basic requirement that he personally needed to understand, not only how much he might reap from an investment, but also more importantly how much he might lose. He believes that he could only ascertain this in the locality where he has lived for much of his adult life.

SUMMARY: Especially in the formative years of a new business, focus on delivering a profit in your home market and on your own doorstep. Once you have achieved that then look further afield.

CHAPTER 38
Financial

'Maybe you know people who make millions of pounds a year, yet don't have fulfilling relationships or good health. Or people who spend their life committed to religion or spirituality, literally touching the divine, but have holes in their shoes. We all know people who have razor-sharp intellects but are ... out of touch. There's a much more integrated, fulfilling way to live: I call it Harmonic Wealth.'

(James Arthur Ray.)

The primary role of the CEO in the corporate world is to increase the financial wealth of the shareholders. This is why s/he is appointed CEO. However, as an individual entrepreneur, the solitary drive to achieve financial success is not necessarily going to lead to happiness and a sense of achievement.

In his book, *Harmonic Wealth*, James Arthur Ray defines wealth as being made up of five pillars or elements: Financial, Relational, Mental, Physical and Spiritual. He explains that each of these carries equal importance, if true Harmonic Wealth is to be attained and enjoyed. For example reflect on how much financial wealth you need. What would you actually do with a very large sum of money? Would you know when to cease taking risks in order to add another million or two to your tally sheet?

According to James Arthur Ray a definition of financial wealth might be: 'that you have enough money and material things in your life that you will no longer waste one precious moment worrying about them.' The 2008 recession has brought what might be labelled the '13th deal' sharply into focus. The number 13 has been chosen because in many cultures it is associated with bad luck. The '13th deal' is the final deal or transaction that brings the house down –a total financial wipeout for you and your family.

Typically, the entrepreneur struggles over a period of time and then arrives at a position in life where s/he has no financial needs, currently or in the foreseeable future, that could not be met from current net assets. Despite that, s/he goes full steam ahead into more transactions and behaves like a headless chicken, buoyed by his/her self-opinionated belief that everything s/he touches turns to gold. S/he is a kind of 'deal junkie'. With the onset of the recession, most of these 'deal junkies' have been financially obliterated.

SUMMARY: If you must pursue larger transactions and more deals, to add to your financial wealth, a little time taken to 'box off' or 'protect' previously acquired financial wealth will save a total meltdown if you enter into a '13th deal'.

CHAPTER 39
Firing the CEO

This is the function of the Board of Directors. It is usually very difficult for the Board to bring themselves to make this decision. It is not unusual for Boards to give public support to the CEO, despite the obvious shortcomings that are fully visible in the public domain. There have been instances where the CEO has received unqualified Board support, despite being found guilty of breaches of Company Law.

The reality is that Directors on most Boards are not independent and are not voted on by an informed majority of shareholders.

The CEO, in collusion with the Chairperson, often has a strangle-hold on the power base within an organisation. The CEO becomes akin to a Dictator, surrounded at the Board table by loyal 'YES MEN or WOMEN'. Where the Chairperson was the former CEO, this intensifies the ineffectiveness of the Board of Directors.

In such instances, the CEO may actually be the puppet of the Chairperson; old, inappropriate activities can continue unabated by the weakened CEO, who is most likely an appointee of the Chairperson. This is a most unhealthy situation and whilst disliked by the institutional investors, their inaction on preventing or objecting to it is unexplainable.

In any event a CEO that has held the position in excess of seven years should be replaced.

SUMMARY: The lack of independence that is commonplace within the Boardroom means the incompetent CEO can survive beyond what might, for example, be tolerated from a manager in a Premiership football club. Clear annual budgets need to be set out, and it should be taken as read, that continuing support for the CEO is conditional on the budgets being achieved.

CHAPTER 40
Firing People

This is one of the most disliked functions within the corporate world. In his book, *Further Up The Organisation*, Robert Townsend states: 'It's a neglected art in most organisations.'

If the employee is not making the grade, after a period of say 12 months, it is better to admit that a mistake was made in hiring them. To procrastinate and not to confront the issue is both unfair to their colleagues, who have to deal with their shortcomings, but also for the employee themselves who might find their 'vocation' in a new environment. Behind the mask of the employee is the human being that has their pride, ego and ambitions.

There are many ways to fire a person. You can simply call them in and tell them to pack up and go and push them out of the organisation that day. Alternatively, you can let the person keep their dignity and explain that the skills, which s/he has, are not appropriate to the 'revamped' function, which may be merged with another function and, regrettably, there is no longer a requirement to retain his/her services.

A third way to fire an employee is by way of 'constructive dismissal'. This is most unpleasant. It can be akin to bullying and usually entails some type of mental pressure being used, that makes the employee feel the need to move onto newer pastures. Beware the line manger that would indulge in such behaviour, as not only will it be seen by the targeted employee but it will also be resented by his/her colleagues.

In assessing the performance of a new employee it is important to recognise that the initial impression can often be wrong and that it can take some time for the new employee to get to grips with the function. The star performer from day one can often fade away over a matter of months, as their work gets sloppy or they become careless.

"Pick a card............any card....."

SUMMARY: It is never an easy or a pleasant task to dismiss a colleague. Care needs to be taken to do it in a manner that is fair and appropriate. Give the employee a reasonable period to get to grips with the function, prior to making the decision to terminate his/her employment.

CHAPTER 41
Franchises

This is a method of utilising a business model that already exists. It usually consists of purchasing the right to operate the distribution of the franchiser's products, techniques and trademarks, in return for a percentage of the weekly or monthly sales. The franchiser normally provides training. Never acquire a franchise from a franchisee, as this could be tantamount to some form of 'pyramid selling' and the 'vendor' will not necessarily be objective.

Franchising is one of the only means available to access venture investment capital, without needing to give up control of the operation in the process. After the brand and formula are carefully designed and properly executed, franchisers are able to sell franchises and expand rapidly across countries and continents, using the capital and resources of their franchisees. They can earn profits whilst greatly reducing the risk and expense that would be inherent in conventional chain operations.

Franchising lends itself to the following enterprises:

- Businesses with a good track record of profitability.
- Businesses built around a unique or unusual concept.
- Businesses with broad geographic appeal.
- Businesses which are relatively easy to operate.
- Businesses which are relatively inexpensive to operate.
- Businesses which are easily duplicated.

The agreement between the Franchiser and the Franchisee is usually a detailed license, for a period from 5 years to 30 years. McDonalds is the largest and most successful franchise in the world.

There are literally thousands of franchises available to be purchased. In choosing one, care needs to be taken so that you do not end up working merely to pay the franchiser's monthly fee.

This can happen, not necessarily as a result of the franchise itself, but as a result of the actual location where you set-up 'shop'. This is particularly so if you are locating, say a Juice Bar in a shopping centre. The product lends itself to impulse buying and, as such, in a busy shopping mall needs to be in a high visibility location, as opposed to some dark corner that has little passing footfall.

"Not much further now, Gran......"

Also, in the rag trade, a franchise in the higher end of the fashion market may be severally disadvantaged by the franchise covenant that the selling price must be consistent in all outlets, across the continent. If all the fashion outlets in your locality are offering a discount whilst you are prevented, then the shoppers will target those neighbouring stores.

SUMMARY: Franchising can offer an 'already-made' business model, with varying levels of support and back-up. Before being overwhelmed by the sales pitch of the franchiser, take time to meet and see the operations of existing operators of that franchise.

CHAPTER 42
Gifts from Suppliers

For the sake of absolute clarity, have it in the employees' terms and conditions of employment that it is the company policy to refuse gifts from suppliers. The contract should articulate that if gifts are received they are to be returned with a note of gratitude and an explanation of the company's policy. Better still, not only include this in the employees' terms, but also include it in the terms of business circulated to each and every supplier and service provider.

Most supplier gifts are innocent and generous gestures of gratitude.

"Oh...and by the way. I Could widen that door for you..."

However, there can be undertones. When the head chef or the purchasing officer receives regular and expensive gifts, assume the worse. The supplier, the head chef and the purchasing officer are screwing the company.

Equally, gifts from the company to customers and suppliers, other than a bottle of 'festive cheer' at Christmas, are to be avoided. Otherwise it is a possible sign to your customers that you have been overcharging them all year.

> **SUMMARY:** A gift is potentially some type of bribe. Best policy is to politely refuse all gifts and not to offer any.

CHAPTER 43
Greed

Greed is the excessive desire for wealth, food and power. It is this greed that makes people rob the old and vulnerable, and loot in emergencies such as flooding, earthquakes and other natural disasters. Greed is the first cousin of selfishness. They usually run hand-in-hand. Selfish people care only about themselves, irrespective of the consequences of this ethos on others.

"Who can put a price tag on corporate greed?"

In the corporate world, the absolute greed and selfishness that can become the hallmark of long-serving CEOs can often convert to larceny and other activities which are highly inappropriate, if not criminal by legal definition. Obtaining financial wealth, by any means, becomes the modus operandi of the greedy and selfish.

Bernie Madoff, in June 2009 was sentenced to 150 years for committing the largest, known fraud on Earth. He operated a Ponzi scheme which ultimately became unstuck. Fuelled by greed, he and his family lived their lives as if they were Arabian oil sheikhs.

In March 2009, Madoff pleaded guilty to 11 federal crimes, including securities fraud, wire fraud, mail fraud, money laundering, perjury and making false returns with the Securities and Exchange Commission (SEC). The plea came in response to a criminal complaint filed two days earlier, which stated Madoff had defrauded his clients of almost $65 billion.

Madoff stated that he began his Ponzi scheme in 1991. He divulged that he had never made any legitimate investments with his clients' money during this time. Instead he simply deposited the money into his Chase Manhattan Bank account. He was committed to satisfying his clients' expectations of high returns, despite an economic recession. He admitted to false trading activities, masked by foreign transfers and false SEC filings. He told the court that his intention had always been to resume legitimate trading activity, but it proved 'difficult, and ultimately impossible' to reconcile his client accounts.

Behind the financial figures, there lies the overwhelming misery brought upon thousands of small investors who entrusted their life savings and pension funds into his care, trusting Madoff's integrity and apparent 'Midas' investment touch. Having fallen victim to his absolute greed and selfishness, some, in absolute despair, have committed suicide.

Another example of greed and selfishness that led to grand larceny is that of the Canadian, Conrad Moffat Black, Baron Black of Crossharbour. He was a historian, columnist and publisher, who was, for a time, the third biggest newspaper magnate in the world. Black controlled Hollinger International, Inc. who published major newspapers including *The Daily Telegraph* (UK), *The Jerusalem Post*, *National Post* (Canada), and hundreds of community newspapers in North America.

In 2007, Black was found guilty and sentenced to serve six and a half years in prison, repay Hollinger $6.1 million and pay a fine of $125,000. He was incarcerated at the Coleman Federal Correctional Complex in Florida. He was also found guilty of diverting funds for personal benefit from money due to Hollinger International, when the company sold certain publishing assets.

This obsession with creating financial wealth and talking about financial wealth can often lead to broken marriages, the loss of family life and the absence of true friends and colleagues.

In my local gym, I regularly come across an attendee who first enquires as to my welfare and then immediately asks about my business activities. Before I get the chance to fully respond, he always interrupts to tell me about his financial wealth and latest money-making venture. I am obliged to listen politely.

I go to the gym to do a physical workout. I am not interested in anyone's business in that environment. I am more interested in the number of calories I burn and, for that matter, might be interested in the number of calories he burns. His extreme obsession with talking about money, and how much he is worth, is a sad reflection of his low self-esteem and insecurity. Since the recession started to bite in the second half of 2008, his absence from the gym is noticeable.

SUMMARY: If you have it, don't flash it, don't boast about it, keep it to yourself. Who cares how much you have?

CHAPTER 44
Growth

An organisation will either grow in terms of turnover or will shrink. In the business world, it would appear that staying stationary is not an option.

There are two types of growth; Organic growth or growth by acquisition; the former, whilst slower, is more certain and less risky, than growth by acquisition.

The McDonalds' burger business began in 1940, with a restaurant opened by brothers Dick and Mac McDonald in San Bernardino, California. Their introduction of the 'Speedee Service System' in 1948, established the principles of the modern fast-food restaurant. The present corporation dates its founding to the opening of a franchised restaurant by Ray Kroc, in Des Plaines, Illinois in 1955, the ninth McDonalds restaurant to open overall.

Kroc later purchased the McDonald brothers' equity in the company and led its world-wide expansion. The company became listed on the public stock markets in 1965. With the expansion of McDonalds into many international markets, the company has become a symbol of globalisation and the spread of the American way of life.

McDonalds' restaurants are found in 119 countries around the world and serve nearly 47 million customers each day. McDonalds operates over 31,000 restaurants worldwide, employing more than 1.5 million people. The company also operates other restaurant brands, such as Piles Café.

Focusing on its core brand, McDonalds began divesting itself of other chains it had acquired during the 1990s, realising that the only satisfactory growth was organic.

* * * *

Ryanair was founded in 1985 and began with a 15-seat Embraer Bandeirante turbo-prop aircraft, flying between Waterford and London Gatwick Airport with the aim of breaking the duopoly on London/ Republic of Ireland flights at that time, held by British Airways and Aer Lingus.

Passenger numbers continued to increase, but the airline generally ran at a loss and, by 1991, was in need of re-structuring. Michael O'Leary was charged with the task of making the airline profitable. He was encouraged to visit the USA to study the 'low fares/no frills' model being used by Southwest Airlines. O'Leary decided that the key to low fares was to implement quick turnaround times for aircraft, 'no frills' and no business class, as well as operating a single model of aircraft.

O'Leary returned from the US, convinced that Ryanair could make huge inroads into the European air market, at that time dominated by inefficient national carriers, which were subsidised, to various degrees, by their parent countries. He competed with these major airlines by providing a 'no-frills', low cost service.

By 1995, after the consistent pursuit of its low cost business model, Ryanair celebrated its 10th birthday by carrying 2.25 million passengers.

Ryanair's revenues have risen from €231 million in 1998, to some €2,942 million for the 12 months ended 31 March 2009. Passenger numbers exceeded 58 million during the same 12 month period to 31 March 2009.

Even those that bad mouth O'Leary and Ryanair cannot deny that European air travel has changed irreversibly for the better as a result of his presence. People in the tourist sectors in Ireland and other Ryanair destinations are very aware of the major contribution the company has made to tourism. The Ryanair success is a fine example of organic growth, with a clear, narrow focus.

On the other hand, growth by acquisition and merger has been the hallmark of Lloyds Bank, one of the oldest banks in the UK, tracing its establishment to Charles Lloyd of Wales in 1677. Through a series of mergers, Lloyds has become one of the Big Four banks in the UK. In 1995, the merger between TSB and Lloyds Bank formed Lloyds TSB Group plc, one of the largest forces in domestic banking. It continued to prosper and bought and sold financial companies over the next decade.

On 17 September 2008, it was reported that HBOS was in takeover talks with Lloyds TSB, in response to a precipitous drop in HBOS's share price. The takeover talks concluded successfully that evening, with a proposal to create a banking giant, that would hold a third of the UK mortgage market.

In February 2009, Lloyds Banking Group revealed that the losses at HBOS, at around £10 billion, were greater than had been anticipated. The share price of Lloyds Banking Group plunged 32% on the London Stock Exchange. The acquisition had been carried out too rapidly and too recklessly. Lloyds subsequently needed an UK Government bailout, effectively diluting the existing shareholders by almost 50%, and is now classified as a 'lame duck bank'.

A similar situation occurred with Royal Bank of Scotland (RBS). In April 2008 it announced a £12 billion rights issue, to shore up its net assets. The bank had realised that it had 'bought a 'pup' in the acquisition of ABN-Amro which would lead to a write down of some £20 billion. In October 2008, the British Government came to the Bank's rescue, with an equity injection of £37 billion making the UK taxpayer the majority shareholder.

The CEO at the time, Sir Freddie Goodwin, was subsequently forced to retire. He was paid compensation way and above his contractual entitlement, causing a furore amongst the British public. A select committee of the House of Commons at Westminster was set up to investigate the circumstances which led to the granting of such a lucrative golden boot. It was largely inconclusive with no real tangible result.

* * * *

The largest car manufacturer in India, Tata Motors Ltd, is largely associated with low cost cars. In 2008 it acquired from Ford the UK luxury brands of Jaguar and Land Rover, for a sum of £1.7billion. Within months, the total Tata Group was verging on insolvency.

In 1993, Wendelin Wiedeking, arrived as CEO at luxury car maker Porsche which was in deep financial trouble. He is credited with saving Porsche from ruin, by streamlining production, cutting costs and introducing new models. He was celebrated as Germany's most successful manager. He had agreed a contractual bonus at the time of his arrival and in 2008 he earned a bonus of €80 million, making him the highest paid executive in Germany.

Wiedeking then wrote a book called *The David Principle*, about David and Goliath struggles in business, after which it appears he lost the plot. He made the fatal error of attempting to take control of VW, which was seven times the size of Porsche. The end result was failure for Porsche and loss of its independence. In 2009 it became the tenth brand in the VW portfolio. Wiedeking, at the age of 56, was forced to retire, albeit with a multi-million golden handshake, as Porsche was merged into VW.

* * * *

Growth by acquisition and merger can potentially reduce shareholders' wealth, rather than increase it. Organic growth should not be reckless, as was the case in the Dublin-based Anglo Irish Bank, which boasted that it was the fastest growing bank in Europe, if not in the world. In 2008, the bank had to be nationalised by the Irish Government, to avoid an Armageddon for the depositors.

In business it is critical to stay focused on your product range or service. Without doubt Ryanair, over the past two decades, is probably the best example of organic growth with the focus clearly fixed on low cost, short-haul air travel. When asked if Ryanair would service the USA to Europe routes Michael O'Leary gave a swift reply:

'Ryanair will never fly the Atlantic route because one can not get there in a Boeing 737, unless one has a very strong tail wind or passengers that can swim the last hour of the flight.'

(Attributed to Michael O'Leary, CEO Ryanair, in *The Little Book of Mick* by Paul Kilduff.)

> **SUMMARY:** There needs to be an understanding as to the limitations of management to control and monitor growth within the organisation. The desire for growth in turnover and growth by geographical spread regularly over-shadows the necessity for profits and a positive cash flow.

CHAPTER 45
Honesty

'Honesty is the rarest wealth anyone can possess and yet all the honesty in the world ain't lawful tender for a loaf of bread.'

(Anonymous)

Honesty and truth need so little rehearsal. Honesty is a simple word but it has huge implications. It is sadly lacking in many organisations. It means telling the truth, the full truth. Beware of the half-truth – you may have gotten hold of the wrong half.

In the UK, the famous novelist Jeffrey Archer was a leading Conservative politician, confidante of Prime Minister Margaret Thatcher, and member of the House of Lords. In July 2001, he faced dishonesty charges arising from his successful 1987 libel action. He was accused of asking his former friend, Ted Francis, to provide him with a false alibi for a night relating to the libel case and of producing fake diary entries to back up his story. Archer had subsequently won £500,000 damages from *The Daily Star*, over the allegations that he had slept with a prostitute.

Lord Archer was found guilty of two charges of perjury and two of perverting the course of justice. The first guilty verdict was that he had perverted the course of justice by asking Ted Francis to give him a false alibi. The second was on a charge that he perverted the course of justice by using a fake diary in the libel trial. Additionally he was found to have perjured himself in an affidavit to the High Court for the libel action. He was also found to have perjured himself on oath during the libel trial.

The multi-millionaire Archer was jailed for four years after being found guilty and ordered to pay £175,000.

In 2010, Judge Peter Kelly in the Dublin High Court in a case involving Ryanair surmised: *'Having considered Ryanair's untruths in the Court and untruths about the Court, one has to conclude that the truth and Ryanair are uncomfortable bedfellows.'*

"I promise to tell the truth, the whole truth and nothing but the truth plus handling charge...'"

SUMMARY: A liar needs a good memory. If you cannot be truthful, be silent. At least you cannot be charged with perjury.

CHAPTER 46
Integrity

A father is explaining integrity and ethics to his son, who is about to go into business.

'Suppose a woman comes in and orders a €100 worth of material. You wrap it up, and you give it to her. She pays you with a €100 note. But as she goes out the door you realise she's given you two €100 notes.

Now, here's where integrity and ethics come in: should you or should you not tell your partner?'

* * * *

No one is perfect. It is a matter of degrees. Having integrity entails doing, on each and every occasion, what is right. It is beyond definition. It is like pornography – you will know it when you see it.

It requires, amongst other things, that you pay your full tax liability, always tell the truth and keep your word, especially when it is inconvenient. The simple reality is that if you have substantially increased your financial wealth and, at the same time, maintained absolute integrity, no-one can take that wealth away from you; not the tax man, not the Government, not some disgruntled shareholder or partner.

There are many examples of financial wealth acquired where integrity was lacking:

Conrad Black, the CEO of Hollinger, who owned a string of the best newspaper titles in the world, was incarcerated in an American prison for six years in 2006 for stealing from fellow shareholders; Bernie Madoff was incarcerated for 150 years in a US prison for stealing some $65 billion from investors in the world's biggest Ponzi scheme.

In another example, my colleague worked with a CEO of a large company who would blatantly deny that he had agreed or committed to something. To him, acting inappropriately was being smart and clever. He was of flawed pedigree and was devoid of integrity. He survived for many years as CEO. Eventually he was found out and the organisation came tumbling down, causing billions of Euro of losses to fellow employees, to thousands of small shareholders and to institutional investors.

SUMMARY: Integrity entails doing what is right and what is fair, irrespective of the cost or consequences. It is the perpetual light of good business practice.

CHAPTER 47
Leadership

*'Set a vision, inspire people, get in the skin of people,
follow that vision, and care for your people and most importantly,
listen with one's mouth closed.'*

(Jack Welch former CEO of GE)

Leadership is an activity, not a role. Personality traits, charisma, power, and influence do not define it. Every company has silent or hidden leaders at front line or mid-level. The task for every company is to identify these leaders and aid in their development.

Antanus Mockus was the Mayor of Bogota, Colombia, between 1994 and 2003. When he took the post, the city had the highest female homicide rate in the Americas and the most road deaths at pedestrian crossings in the world. He quickly discovered that the status quo needed to be challenged and started some new initiatives to improve the situation. The city started to hire mime artists to walk across the pedestrian crossings to enlighten the city about the crossings' purpose. The first few artists took a belt of a car or truck in the early days but this initiative brought about a 50% reduction in road deaths at pedestrian crossings. Mockus raised the awareness, with his smart thinking and leadership activities.

He also introduced a girls' night out initiative. For one night a week throughout the city men were put under curfew, in order for the women of the city to enjoy a night out in relative safety. This saw the homicide rate fall by 70% inside the first year.

Leadership is the ability to mobilise people to address the tough problems – those they would rather avoid – and Mockus has shown this in his 10 years in Bogota.

'In a society where human life has lost value, there cannot be a higher priority than re-establishing respect for life.'

(Antanus Mockus)

Sir Alex Ferguson is an example in how to lead and adapt to change. Not only is he a master in leadership but he has the ability to adapt his team and 'move with the change' in order to maintain success for the Club. He challenges his own status quo and manages conflict in a way that has seen Paul McGrath, David Beckam, Rudd Van Nistelrooy and Roy Keane exit the club. 'There is nobody bigger than the club,' is a favourite quote from Ferguson.

Sir Alex uses the 'boil a frog' philosophy, which simply put, suggests that 85% of everything is hard to change and will resist change but the other 15% can be changed. If you target the 15% that can be changed each year, (which in his case is two players) and concentrate on that, another 15% can be changed the following year without creating too much fuss. Hence Sir Alex has changed a successful team every year and doesn't allow complacency to set in within it. If you put a frog in a pot of boiling hot water and leave the lid off, it will surely jump right out. If you put a frog in a pot of cold water, with the lid off, and slowly turn up the heat, then the frog gets comfortable in the pot and will slowly boil.

A strong combination of personal humility and professional will are required to be a great leader. Herb Kelleher, CEO of Southwest Airlines (SWA), is an excellent example. This may explain why SWA are listed in the 'Top 10 companies to work for in the USA'. SWA have been the only consistently profitable airline in the US for the last 20 years. They offer a low cost fare, with a strong focus on customer service. Whilst Michael O'Leary may have modelled Ryanair on the low cost aspect of SWA operations, he was unable to grasp that customer service played a vital role in that airline's success.

Herb Kelleher states that, when picking a team to work around you, it should be on the following basis. 'Hire for attitude and train for skill.'

SUMMARY: Without leadership, enterprises will neither prosper nor adapt to change. It is a quality that is embedded within the person. It is a fully 'rounded' approach to all aspects of the enterprise. It is sadly absent in the political world, as power tends to be grabbed through cronyism and patronage, with little regard to the greater good.

CHAPTER 48
Litigation

As a rule of thumb, do not litigate. The outcome of litigation is not necessarily just and fair. It is the decision of a judge who is not infallible. It is not necessarily based on a proper interpretation of the law of the land. It can be prejudiced by inconsequential issues, such as the demeanour of one of the parties, the personal experience or misunderstanding of the facts by the judge, favouritism, racialism or even corruption.

Before you get involved in litigation, exhaust every avenue for dialogue. Always try to exclude your legal advisors from such negotiations. Enter discussions on a 'without prejudice' basis. Such negotiations need to be: 'principal to principal.'

If, despite your best efforts to reach a compromise, litigation is inevitable, work out the financial consequences of the judgement going against you. You can expect that legal fees will be an additional 40% on top of any award against you. You can take it that, at best, your chances of winning in Court are 50%.

If you are an individual, you might give some thought to the financial effect on your personal assets, in the event that the judgement is against you. By forward planning, you may be able to arrange a damage limitation exercise by transferring a proper and justifiable amount of your assets to your spouse or children. It may be too late to do this once the legal papers have been served.

As for the motivation of your legal team and their advice that you have a strong winnable case, I recall the story below:

Some years ago, Patrick called into his local solicitor to explain that he was going to litigate against one of his neighbours. His solicitor declined to act for Patrick, as he was already acting for the neighbour. He proposed that he would write a note of introduction for Patrick to bring to a fellow solicitor in the neighbouring town.

Patrick went home and explained the situation to his wife.

She insisted that the letter of introduction be opened so they could see its contents.

Reluctantly, Patrick agreed and opened the letter of introduction, which read:

'Dear Colleague, two fat geese. You pluck one, I'll pluck the other.'

> **SUMMARY:** The temptation to litigate is often encouraged by solicitors that are either mercenary or incompetent or both. Litigation has to be the last option, after everything else has failed. In certain circumstances it may be cheaper to concede defeat rather than becoming adsorbed in years of swearing affidavits and complying with court orders for discovery.

CHAPTER 49
Management Information

Information for management in the business organisation should be supplied in the briefest of formats, adequate to flag the essentials and with enough detail to provoke a response. It should be cheap to produce and should be current and completely up-to-date. It should highlight the key issues of actual profits versus budgeted, with the variance labelled either positive or negative. And to keep life as simple as possible, it should be understood that a positive variance is good for the organisation and a negative variance is bad for the organisation. All figures, where relevant, should be compared to budget and to last year's financials. Short, factual reasons for the positive or negative variances should be included.

The section dealing with cash flow should also show the trends in debtors' days and creditors' days. In most businesses, debtors that are over 90 days outstanding from the payment due date, need to be considered as a total bad debt and provided for accordingly; otherwise there needs to be some compelling evidence, such as a bank guarantee, to treat them as receivables.

Management information is primarily to generate action. The test of the quality of both the information and of the management itself is to gauge the response to the negative variances.

The sale and installation of Management Information Systems is a major business within itself. The availability of 'micro-management' information from these expensive systems can, in itself, be a negative for the organisation. The result is often an 'information overload' with the key critical aspects of the report getting lost in the abundance of content.

SUMMARY: Look carefully at the volume and quality of information being provided. Information needs to be the catalyst that forces line managers into action, to correct the negative variances. Otherwise the information has no real benefit.

CHAPTER 50
Management Meetings

These are necessary in order to communicate with different departments. Do not have the meetings in the Boardroom, with all the frills of refreshments and especially do not provide lunch.

Have all Heads of Departments meet at the reception desk each morning, 15 minutes before the official start time. It will remove the mystique and prestige of being an attendee at the daily management meeting and you will be amazed how the focus will be fixed on important and relevant issues.

Minutes will not be necessary. Unless there is a pandemic of Alzheimer's within the attendees, decisions will not be forgotten, given the frequency of the meetings.

SUMMARY: Internal management meetings are generally a waste of time and a disruption to the normal workings of the organisation. Keep meetings to the bare minimum and let brevity be the order of the day.

117

CHAPTER 51
Marketing Consultants

Unlike PR consultants, marketing consultants have a use. Select the firm, or preferably the individual, who has not worked for a competitor in the past five years. Brief him/her fully on your company products, the company ethos and the objectives you would hope to achieve from a marketing spend.

Explain that the consultants may elicit any information, from any member of the senior management. When the presentation is ready, it can be demonstrated to the management team who will either accept it outright or reject it outright. Make it clear to the management team that they cannot tinker with it. In other words, you are not hiring in marketing consultants and at the same time accepting the proposals on an 'á la carte' basis.

It is occasionally useful to take the senior managers and line mangers to a hotel, including an overnight stay, to focus their minds fully on the marketing objectives. The location should be as close as possible to base but of a good quality and in the seclusion of the countryside. It is not a good idea to turn it into a 'junket' by opting for some exotic place half-way around the world.

Good ideas can emanate from such gatherings, so long as each of the attendees is aware that it is projects that are workable and can be implemented without unnecessary disruption to the current business, which are being sought. A synergy can develop amongst participants and, loath as I am to use the phrase, a bit of 'brainstorming' can yield interesting results.

SUMMARY: Marketing is a function that needs input from the CEO and initiatives need to be implemented in a manner that allows for a resulting increase in sales to be assessed. Avoid a situation of all marketing but no selling.

CHAPTER 52
Mental Wealth

'A man is but the product of his thoughts.
What he thinks, he becomes.'

(Mahatma Gandhi)

In his book, Harmonic Wealth, James Arthur Ray emphasises the need to open up and control one's mind. Ray explains that doing so will assist you to open up yourself to achieving a life of abundance and contentment, free from feelings of dissatisfaction and insecurity.

Many people pay little attention to the choices they make about how they wish to live their lives. They are constrained by their perceived circumstances – they are drifters. Ambitions are suppressed, in favour of expediency. Such lack of focus steals dreams, and creates misery.

'Bogged down in limiting and negative thoughts while the things they really want to attend to are put off week after week, they give over their lives to routines and responsibilities while their hopes and dreams slip through their fingers.'

(James Arthur Ray)

SUMMARY: It is easy to get consumed in the day-to-day workings of your business and lose sight of the bigger picture – stand back and look in; take control. Move over from the passenger's seat to that of the driver's. Why choose failure when success is an option?

CHAPTER 53
Mitsakes!

*'Are we going to apologise when something goes wrong?
No, we're f***ing not.'*

(Attributed to Michael O'Leary, CEO Ryanair,
in *The Little Book of Mick* by Paul Kilduff.)

Mistakes can be made by intemperate or badly thought out public comment. Gerard Ratner joined the family jewellery business in 1966 and as CEO he built up a successful chain of jewellers during the 1980s. The shops were an affront to the formerly staid jewellery industry. They displayed fluorescent, orange posters, advertising cut price bargains and offered low price ranges.

Although widely regarded as 'tacky', the shops and their wares were nevertheless extremely popular with the public, that is until Ratner made a speech at an Institute of Directors' function in 1991. During the speech, he announced: 'We also do cut-glass sherry decanters, complete with six glasses on a silver-plated tray that your butler can serve you drinks on, all for £4.95. People say, "How can you sell this for such a low price?" I say, "Because it's total crap."'

Ratner compounded this by going on to remark that some of the earrings were: 'cheaper than an M&S prawn sandwich but probably wouldn't last as long.' After the speech, the value of the Ratner's group plummeted by around £500 million, which very nearly resulted in the firm's collapse.

Today, Ratner's speech is still famous in the corporate world. Such gaffes are now sometimes called 'Doing a Ratner'. In his own defence, he has said that it was a private function, which he did not expect to be reported, and his remarks were not made seriously.

It is equally important to encourage managers down the line of command, to admit to mistakes, discuss them and to introduce a protocol to avoid the same mistake being made again.

A sign of weakness and incompetence is the divisional manager or head of a department attempting to lay the blame for an error on one of their subordinates, which is a way of distracting from their own shortcomings. Managers need to be reminded that in business the objective is to learn from a mistake and to prevent its repeat – not to allocate blame, which achieves nothing.

SUMMARY: It is not possible to operate and grow a business without making mistakes. It is the inability to recognise the mistake and to accept responsibility for it that is the real concern. When the CEO of an organisation makes a mistake, s/he should admit to it and talk about it freely to colleagues. Learn from mistakes. If you are not making mistakes you are not trying.

CHAPTER 54
Mistresses

When speaking on the subject with my colleague, he remarked:
'It would be impossible for me to have a mistress as I talk in my sleep.'

Having a mistress is the ultimate distraction for a male business leader or senior executive in an organisation. The cost and commitment of keeping two women is much more than twice the cost and commitment of keeping one. It requires deceit, cunning and a bag-full of extra energy.

If the activity is outside the organisation, there is little that can be said or done but, sooner or later, the productivity and focus of the executive or CEO will falter. It is when the organisation is suffering, that action will have to be taken to help the individual to move out of the company to continue his career elsewhere.

It is even more disruptive if the pair work within the same organisation. The first signs of such an in-house relationship can be detected if a pattern emerges of after-hours working or working at the weekends, when the business is officially closed. Also you might notice a more generous pay review for a particular person or a bonus above what could reasonably be expected. An increase in activity in the CEO's expense account is also likely.

Despite secrecy and discretion by both parties, it will be known quickly within the organisation that the CEO is having an affair.

Action has to be taken by the Chairperson and again the CEO needs to be confronted and assisted to move to another company. As for his partner, usually of junior ranking, the best solution is to help her relocate to another organisation.

"Johnson..It's a big mistake to think you can sweep your affair under the carpet!'"

The most powerful man in the world in 1998, President Bill Clinton, was reported to be having a sexual relationship with Monica Lewinsky, a 22-year-old intern employed at the White House. The news of this extra-marital affair, and his sworn denial of such, resulted in a special investigation, which eventually led to an impeachment hearing in 1998 by the US House of Representatives.

Clinton was subsequently acquitted on all impeachment charges of perjury and obstruction of justice in a 21-day Senate trial. Ultimately, it did not take away from Clinton's worldwide popularity, but the life of Monica Lewinsky will be tainted forever by the detailed evidence that was made public during this period.

In a subsequent poll, 1,000 'eligible' American females were asked if they would have an affair with Bill Clinton. A total of 990 responded: 'never again!'

In January 2010, it was revealed that the football player attempting to gag the press from publishing details of his alleged affair was Chelsea and England captain, John Terry. It was alleged that Terry, who had married in 2007, had had an affair with Vanessa Perroncel, while she was the girlfriend of his team-mate, Wayne Bridge. This could only complicate matters for the England coach, Fabio Capello, as he prepared the team for the World Cup in South Africa. Terry was dropped as the England team captain.

Another superstar sportsman and one of the world's greatest golfers, Tiger Woods, emerged as a serial adulterer following a 'traffic' incident at his home in December 2009. Woods immediately went into hiding and withdrew from several golf tournaments. By the end of January 2010, sponsors of Woods began to cancel their contracts, as it was deemed inappropriate to have an association with such an unsuitable role model. Woods, who had married Elin Nordgren in October 2004, stands to lose millions of dollars as a result of his infidelity and lack of judgement.

SUMMARY: There is no such thing as an extra-marital relationship without consequences. It is not possible in the workplace to conceal such a relationship. Apart from the human issues and complications, it is a major source of distraction for the executive and his performance at work. A policy statement setting out the corporate intolerance of such relationships, whilst not legally enforceable, can act as a reminder to all involved that it is unacceptable.

CHAPTER 55
Nepotism

The CEO of a large public company sent for his personnel manager and told her: 'My son will be graduating from engineering college next month. I want you to take him on as your assistant. But mind you, I don't want you to show any favouritism towards him. Treat him as you would treat any of my other sons.'

Nepotism can be defined as 'business or political patronage bestowed, or favouritism shown, on the basis of family or romantic relationship.'

Take this example: Paul Wolfowitz, who had been appointed Head of the World Bank in June 2005, had to resign in May 2007, after being accused of arranging a large salary increase and a promotion for one Shaha Riza, a junior work colleague with whom he was having a relationship.

Nepotism in the workplace can act as a de-motivational influence on other employees. Yet most employers deny it exists at all. In the corporate sector, favouritism, as it is commonly known, occurs when someone appears to be treated better than others and it's not necessarily due to their superior work performance. This unfair advantage can lead to feelings of resentment and mistrust, resulting in decreased morale and productivity.

Nepotism may result in the unfair promotion of less efficient people, ahead of those who are more qualified. Often they are paid more to do the same job as others, given more flexibility in working hours and receive other benefits. Under a regime of nepotism, opportunity blossoms as a result of whom you know, irrespective of your capabilities. The instances of favouring a family member are widely seen and, to a large extent, accepted in family-controlled businesses.

In June 2002, Anthony O'Reilly, CEO of Independent News and Media, a public-quoted company, was questioned by a shareholder on the issue of nepotism, following the appointment of his son Gavin as Chief Operating Officer.

"I don't want to spoil my son. He starts here tomorrow, but don't promote him for at least two weeks."

The shareholder said Sir Anthony owned 27% of the company – but the remaining 73% of shareholder interests must be considered. He quoted an article from *The Economist* saying that family involvement in companies is bad for shareholders, and he called on the other Directors to look at this issue.

Anthony O'Reilly was unrepentant, saying the right man got the job. 'The issue of nepotism,' he said, 'will never go away.' He cited Heinz as an example where he, O'Reilly, was one of six Chief Executives – the other five were all Heinzes. 'Family lines,' he said, 'should not disqualify.'

If Gavin O'Reilly was that good, he should have gone off and proven it somewhere else. Since 2002, the fortunes of the Independent News and Media Group have plummeted and by the third quarter of 2009 the organisation was technically insolvent, with a huge overhang of debt by way of bonds and bank finance. It is doubtful now if Anthony O'Reilly's son Gavin, was the 'right man for the job'.

> **SUMMARY:** The 'right man or woman for the job' may well be one of the family but this should be evidenced by the success and reputation they have gained working for a third party or unconnected employer. After this demonstration of success, family lines should not disqualify.

CHAPTER 56
Objectives

An objective is defined as: 'A mission, purpose, or standard that can be reasonably achieved within the expected timeframe and with the available resources.'

Objectives are the most basic components underlying all planning and strategic activities. They serve as the basis for policy and performance appraisals, and act as the glue that binds the entire organisation together.

Making profits is not an objective in itself but is a reward for delivering on proper or well thought out objectives. Every business and every entrepreneur needs to have objectives. The commercial objective needs to be articulated clearly and concisely. It needs to be short and to the point. It must be capable of being written down but short enough to be memorised.

When Robert Townsend became CEO of Avis Rent-a-Car in 1962, he set about changing the direction and culture of that organisation, as Avis was trailing in the hierarchy behind Hertz. Townsend's simple objective was: 'to become the fastest growing company, with the highest profit margins in the business of renting and leasing vehicles without drivers.'

With the acceptance of this statement, it was easy to divest Avis of the limousine and sight-seeing companies which it already owned and which required drivers. It also made it easy to reject offers to expand by for example, acquiring hotels, travel companies and airlines. It was now the key focus of the CEO to deliver on these objectives and not to waste time on side issues. Unlike many organisations which take on the conglomerate mentality of doing a little bit of everything – a total lack of concentration.

Robert Townsend went on to pen the business book, *Up the Organisation* in 1970, which became a bestseller. It brought 'no nonsense' clarity to the world of business and business decisions. Those executives and CEOs that have read it will have benefited greatly from his experience and common sense approach to running an organisation.

"If you isolate the ambition gene in the next half hour, can I have it in my coffee?'"

For the individual, life can roll on, day after day, with no purpose or meaning. There can be an underlying unhappiness, fuelling stress and anxiety. There is a simple solution – try to identify your individual ambitions and objectives, covering all aspects of your life. When thought through, try and summarise them in writing. Keep it simple and brief. Remember the Barrack Obama motto: 'Yes, we can.' He said it; he did it, and so can you.

SUMMARY: With your objectives in mind, every day and every hour of that day, ask yourself if your action is getting you any closer to your objectives. If not, try again and try harder. If you don't try, you can never make it. It's like the Lotto: the odds of winning by doing it are almost equal to the odds of winning it by not doing it, even so – if you are not in you cannot win.

CHAPTER 57
Offices

Various members of an organisation's hierarchy will attach importance to the size, location and furnishings in their office. All offices should be the same minimum size, with exactly the same furnishings and with a maximum of two extra seats for meeting visitors and customers.

Ideally there should be no individual offices, with everyone working in an open-plan environment. This is generally more efficient and provides less opportunity for an employee to conduct personal business and waste time on idle chat. Also, an unhealthy hierarchy can be created simply by the allocation of offices, in the same way that reserved parking for management can contribute to it.

SUMMARY: Discourage managers and executives from being focused on unimportant things like the size or location of their office: Lead by example.

CHAPTER 58
Organisation Charts

There are conflicting views on the need or desirability for definitive organisation charts. Modern thinking suggests that these should be flat and not the traditional pyramid. It is also suggested that the management structure should be circular.

It has yet to be shown how the workings of an organisation might be explained to a potential investor without the aid of a pyramid type organisation chart. It is not an unreasonable objective within an organisation that each employee reports to a single superior. Otherwise total chaos might ensue, with different superiors issuing different and possibly contradictory instructions to subordinates. For salary reviews, organisation charts can bring a logical approach to wage differentials. Also, an organisation chart is invaluable when allocating and identifying responsibilities.

"I'm sorry Simpkins, but 'eeney, meeny, miney, mo' is no solution to where the buck should stop....."

Some organisations are so tiered it is not easy for the lay person to fathom how they are structured. Take the case of the Catholic Priest and a Jewish Rabbi who were chatting one day when the conversation turned to a discussion of job descriptions and the future:

'What position do you see for yourself in a couple years from now?' asked the Rabbi to the Priest.

'Well, actually, I'm next in line for the Monsignor's job,' replied the Priest.

'Yes, and then what?' asked the Rabbi.

'Well, I could become Auxiliary Bishop,' said the Priest.

'Yes, and then?' asked the Rabbi.

'Well, if I work real hard and do a good job it's possible to become a full Bishop,' said the Priest.

'Okay, then what?' continued the Rabbi.

The Priest, beginning to be a bit exasperated replied: 'With some luck and real hard work, maybe I can become an Arch-Bishop. And then,' continued the priest, 'possibly a Cardinal.'

'And then?' continued the Rabbi.

The Priest is really starting to get frustrated, but replies, 'With lots and lots of luck and some real difficult work and, if I'm in the right place, at the right time, and play my political games just right, maybe, just maybe, I can get elected Pope.'

'Yes, and then what?' continued the Rabbi.

'Good grief!' shouted the Priest, 'What do you expect me to become, God?'

'Well,' said the Rabbi, 'one of our boys made it!'

SUMMARY: The more layers within the organisation, the greater the necessity to have it set out in a chart identifying the reporting structure and where responsibility lies.

CHAPTER 59
Outside Directorships

If the CEO accepts outside non-executive directorships and honorary positions with trade or professional organisations, be on the alert. If s/he has that much time and energy to spare, it means the organisation is over-staffed. It is common practice for many CEOs to take cross-directorships with companies which often have multiple common Directors with each other's organisations. It becomes a 'Club of Fellow Directors'.

Some CEOs like giving advice or making speeches on topics they generally know nothing about instead of being in their place of employment, minding the business of their shareholders. Take the case of Gerard Ratner. He was at an Institute of Directors' function bad-mouthing his own products and causing the near collapse of the business that paid him his salary.

> **SUMMARY:** It's time to fire the CEO who feels the need, has the time or has the inclination, to be available to join this circle of time-wasters. S/he has lost their way.

CHAPTER 60
Overpaid

In 2007, Jonathan Ross became the highest paid television presenter in the UK. A new BBC contract secured his services until 2010, for a reported £18 million, equivalent to £6 million per annum. The BBC is fully funded by the British taxpayer, through an archaic tax known as a TV license fee. It is a legal requirement in the UK that each household that has a TV receiver must pay an annual tax. The BBC does not air commercial ads nor accept sponsorships.

Subsequently on 29 October, following an appearance by Ross on *The Russell Brand Show* broadcast in October 2008, Ross was suspended by the BBC for 12 weeks without pay. This was after a series of lewd and inappropriate phone messages were left for the 79-year-old actor Andrew Sachs by Brand and Ross and broadcast on the pre-recorded show.

There was minimal reaction initially but a media story about the calls generated a high number of complaints. Brand resigned from the BBC, while Ross was suspended. BBC Director General Mark Thompson stated that Ross should take the disciplinary action as a 'final warning'. The BBC was later fined £150,000 by Britain's broadcast regulator for airing the calls.

* * * *

In Ireland, its bankers enjoyed multi-million Euro remuneration packages during the first decade of the new millennium. Despite such large rewards, the recipients have generally proven to be incompetent and the banking sector has had to be rescued by the Irish taxpayer and the European Central Bank.

Again, Irish politicians were some of the highest paid in Europe and the first minister, an Taoiseach, enjoyed a remuneration greater than that of the US President. Not withstanding such generous payments, the competency levels of the recipients was very low. And again the Irish Republic has had to be rescued from financial default by the International Monetary Fund and the European Union.

"Tell me.....Where do you see yourself five years ago?......."

SUMMARY: The reality has been that large remunerations do not necessarily buy skill, intelligence or competency. A further negative has been the differential in pay rates between senior executives and line workers in many western economies. It has little justification and fails to recognise the necessary contribution of the line workers. Such differentials are a source of justified discontent to the Trade Unions.

CHAPTER 61
Partnerships

A partnership is a type of business entity in which two or more owners, referred to as partners, share with each other the profits or losses of the business. It is usually organised under a 'Partnership Agreement' which specifies the procedures to settle issues and for decision-making. It will include rules to deal with profits or losses, contributions to the Partners' Capital Account, and the action to be taken in the event that one or more of the partners is unable to perform his/her duties, as a result of long-term illness, imprisonment or bankruptcy.

Partnerships traditionally have been the favoured operational entity for the professions – accountants, auditors, architects, medical doctors and lawyers. They are often favoured over limited liability companies or corporations for taxation purposes. The partnership structure does not generally incur a tax on profits before it is distributed to the partners. However, depending on the partnership structure and the national laws under which it operates, owners of a partnership may be exposed to unlimited personal liability, which would be greater than the liability they might face as company shareholders. With an increasingly litigious clientele and the escalating cost of Professional Indemnity Insurance, more and more of the professions are organising themselves into some type of limited liability entity.

As an operational entity, the Partnership model is fraught with difficulties. The traditional pyramid organisation chart cannot apply, as there are many owners and it is difficult to empower one partner with the role of CEO. As the partnership grows in both size and profitability, an increasing level of resentment ferments, not only between the partners themselves but it is regularly fuelled by their spouses' opinions on the level of effort and commitment put into the 'practice' by each individual.

At retirement age, unless there is a well thought out and fair procedure to value the goodwill of the retiring partner, another source of conflict and bad feeling can ensue.

> **SUMMARY:** As a general rule, partnerships are to be avoided on a number of fronts.

CHAPTER 62
Political Donations

Companies traditionally made political donations to a particular political party in order to have influence over policies that might affect their products and services. It is always easier to get the ear of the relevant Government Minister if you have funded his party's political machine to the tune of several thousand Euro. Attending political fund-raising lunches and dinners comes under the same umbrella.

Another reason, and probably the more prevalent, for expending the company's resources on political donations, is to be in the running for a ministerial appointment to some State Board or Quango, or in the UK to the House of Lords. The much sought after prestige of these appointments is a contagious disease amongst CEOs and company Chairpersons.

"No favours sought or given, but consider re-branding"

SUMMARY: The motives for making political donations are always suspect. The Board of Directors that approves such frivolous spending as political donations should be brought to heel by the shareholders, if the information is disclosed.

CHAPTER 63
Physical Wealth

You do have it within your power to contribute positively and significantly to your physical well being. Within the Company, the CEO's or the senior executives' rapidly expanding waistlines, can be an amber, flashing light, to indicate that all is not well. The lack of regard for physical well being, both in personal presentation and physique, does not bode well for the future. In the case of the armed services, you do not see the officers badly dressed and out of physical shape. It simply would not be in harmony with the perceived requirements of the job.

The same is also true in all aspects of business. Healthy body, healthy mind is more than a catch-phrase. Unhealthy executives cannot deliver their best. Most likely they are a burden on their colleagues who, as a result, have to work harder to cover for them.

The flashing, amber light can indicate an increased reliance on booze, or that the friendship of food is necessary to distract from other issues. It is not conducive to have the senior staff out of shape and probably out of energy.

> **SUMMARY:** Lack of awareness of your physical presence and lack of continuous conscientiousness that you are what you eat, will ultimately be detrimental to your ability to deliver on your business objectives.

CHAPTER 64
PR Consultants

If you are capable of telling the truth in a straight-forward and uncomplicated manner, it is surprising that your organisation needs a Public Relations (PR) consultant. In general, these consultants will not know your business better than the senior management team and, as such, the ability of the PR consultant to articulate correctly and accurately is suspect.

"Maybe we wouldn't be in this mess if you'd told the truth for once!....""

SUMMARY: If you have a genuine product or service, why do you need PR consultants? If for some reason negative news is broadcast about the organisation, respond with the truth. It will eventually come out, irrespective of the spin a PR consultant might care to release. Have all the senior management team designated as respondents to media enquiries.

CHAPTER 65
Procrastination

'Procrastination is opportunity's assassin.'

(Victor Kian)

Procrastination is the grave in which opportunity is buried. It is the bad habit of putting off until the day after tomorrow, what should have been done the day before yesterday.

The road to hell is lined with good intentions. 'Putting off until tomorrow' is a common illness, afflicting the 'spent' executive or CEO. It is a reflection of gross inefficiency and laziness. It can have dire consequences where dynamic management is required to meet the challenges of the modern business.

Procrastination is more recognisable in those organisations that are in perpetual financial difficulty because of the inability of the management to tackle the issues, once and for all. As far back as 1985, the world famous Waterford Crystal glass company commenced a programme of selling off non-core businesses, such as the Renault motor import and distribution business and its small ticket, credit lending businesses. This was part of its rationalisation programme.

For the next 23 years, successive and expensive re-structuring programs were introduced, involving difficult negotiations with trade unions and the outsourcing of crystal glass production to Eastern Europe. It was a slow death, until eventually, in 2008, the inevitable closure of the facility in Waterford, Ireland, became the reality.

It was no surprise that the only value left was the actual Waterford Crystal brand name itself. This should have been obvious to the management for the 20 years preceding its collapse. Various CEOs and Boards of Directors procrastinated and eventually the opportunity to salvage something for the work force and shareholders had passed.

In Europe today, virtually all the 'National' airlines are sitting out the final days of trading, under weak, ineffective and inefficient managers. The recently privatised Aer Lingus, Ireland's former flag-carrier, has had several cost-cutting and efficiency re-structuring sessions. However, there has been procrastination by the Board and by various CEOs, a refusal to 'take the bull by the horns'. The reluctance, or inability, to perform the necessary but difficult tasks of removing all outdated work practices, bringing remuneration into line with that of its competitors and reducing gross over-staffing, particularly at management grades, will ultimately lead to the demise into oblivion of this airline.

SUMMARY: Do not procrastinate. In your organisation, identify the procrastinators. They will miss many opportunities to enhance the business. It is best to help them to re-locate to a new employer.

CHAPTER 66
Profits

If you wish to remain in business you simply must make profits. Not only must you make profits but you must also generate a positive cash flow. It is not rocket science. Making profits does not necessarily mean you can remain in business. Cash flow is the umbilical cord that maintains solvency.

Sometimes the definition of profits is suspect. Take a simple example of the haulier who owns the single truck. Not only must the daily revenue cover the daily costs, such as insurance, fuel, maintenance, tolls and incidentals but it must also provide a 'sinking fund' so that the truck can be replaced at the end of its economic life. The standard depreciation charge is rarely adequate to take into account inflation, specifically in new truck prices, or the cost associated with complying with the ever increasing mechanical and environmental requirements of the EU and Central Governments.

SUMMARY: If you have a profitable business, with a positive cash flow, then you have the essential ingredient for sustainability. A business with one without the other simply cannot continue indefinitely, unless there is continuous financial support from outside, such as the shareholders.

CHAPTER 67
Promotions

The first place to look to fill a vacancy in the organisation is from within. There are simple, practical reasons for doing this; firstly, the insider has the minimal learning curve to get to grips with the new job; secondly, their capabilities are already known; thirdly, and most importantly, their weaknesses are already known; fourthly, if you parachute in an outsider, to fill each and every vacant position, it will quickly send a message to existing staff that they are inferior and will be overlooked if an opportunity arises to progress. This will demoralise your good employees, who will in turn seek to progress their careers within another organisation, leaving you with the slackers. You will easily identify the person in the organisation who is already a success and is hungry for more responsibility. Overcome the reluctance to 'rock the boat', by promoting the accomplished performer in one role to a new one.

The alternative is to hire a complete outsider and spend the next six months explaining the job to them. At the end of that period, the reality that you have been 'sold a pup' will have struck home. Then the unpleasant task of firing the new employee will have to be undertaken.

> **SUMMARY:** Be careful not to rush to judgement on an individual before assessing them thoroughly for promotion. Opportunities for advancement within an organisation should be the incentive for employees to put in their best effort on a continuous basis. Whilst 'fresh blood' can be beneficial to an organisation, it can also act as a disincentive for the existing staff.

CHAPTER 68
Phone Calls

Phones, and even more so with the introduction of the mobile phone, mean that you can virtually always be contacted. However, there is a time and place for receiving calls. Taking calls in the middle of a meeting with colleagues is most inappropriate and downright rude. It disrupts your colleagues' thought processes and is most unprofessional.

"Those in favour of banning mobiles from
our meetings, text 'no' to 086 835..........."

SUMMARY: In such situations, turn your phone off or have it redirected to the central switch, where the caller can be told that you will return the call later that day.

CHAPTER 69
Pulling the Plug

The company's inability to recognise failure or defeat, changing fashions or tastes or the inability to recognise the dead horse or white elephant has caused mayhem in many organisations.

Robert Townsend suggests that in every organisation, one senior executive should have the additional mandate of being responsible for closing down loss-making elements, be they individual product lines or whole divisions. The continuing operation of loss-making elements within the organisation may be as a result of a 'head in the sand' approach by the CEO. It may even be for humane reasons, such as not wishing to make employees redundant.

In the media industry there are numerous examples of loss-making divisions or newspaper titles that have been making losses for decades. But for some unexplainable reason, they are allowed to continue trading. The UK *Independent* newspaper racked up million pound losses each year, and in Ireland, the *Sunday Tribune*, which had not made a profit in 20 years, accumulated losses to the order of €50m. Eventually, the *Independent* was sold for a nominal amount and the *Sunday Tribune* closed and was put into liquidation in 2010. INM Group PLC owned both newspapers for many years. In 2009, the parent company itself was on the brink of insolvency, due to its inability to repay or re-finance bondholder debt.

> **SUMMARY:** Each, and every, trading division within an organisation needs to make a contribution to the fixed costs. If not, why not? Re-energise it, refocus it or close it.

CHAPTER 70
Raising Investment

Circulating a 'prospectus' to potential investors is a regular way for companies to try to raise investment. There can be strict legal rules governing such a solicitation. In the smaller company or enterprise, fund-raising documents regularly have a cautionary note, declaring that indeed the document is not a 'prospectus'.

Fund-raising documents should set out on the very first page:

- The amount of funds being raised.

- The method under which they are being raised; be it, for equity, for a bond or some other instrument.

- The purpose to which the funds are being applied.

- The percentage shareholding and expected return to investors.

Often the potential investor has to wade through page after page of detail and, at the end of the ordeal, is none the wiser about what exactly is being sought and what is being given in return.

A very important element in appraising a fund-raising proposal is the ability to clearly identify the Directors behind the venture and to assess their track record to date. The details should be verifiable and need to be specific, not just general comment.

Fundamentally, the business model of the fund-seeking company needs to be articulated clearly and fully understood by potential investors. In the case of ISTC plc, founded in 2005 by Tiarnan O' Mahony, high net worth individuals invested millions of Euro, not necessarily in the company itself, but on the reputation of Tiarnan. He had been the Chief Operating Officer in Anglo Irish Bank, at that stage perceived to be very successful, but had been overlooked in favour of David Drumm for the role of CEO. In 2007, ISTC plc subsequently collapsed, with a loss of €850 million. Many of the people who had invested simply never took the time to understand the business model and potential risks involved.

Interestingly, in May 2007, six months prior to the collapse of ISTC plc, an independent rating agency concluded that the company had the following strengths and challenges:

- A relatively low risk profile with regard to credit and market risk.
- Adhering to regulated banking procedures and policies despite not being a regulated entity.
- Experienced management team, with extensive knowledge of the industry.
- Good liquidity, incorporating some shock absorption capacity.
- Adequate capitalisation, given the low risk profile.

SUMMARY: Boring and all as this may sound, never be too concerned about the profits that might be generated from a particular investment. Profits will take care of themselves. Spend a little time understanding how much you might lose. And how such a loss could impact on your wealth and future financial security. Also, be certain that you understand the business model and are not overwhelmed by the personalities of the promoters.

CHAPTER 71

Relationship Wealth

'Become the person that you want to attract. If it is romantic love you want, be romantic. Want someone with a great body? Go to the gym. Desire a compassionate partner? Be compassionate. Seek someone with a great sense of humour? Lighten up. Do you want friends who are loyal and true? Be loyal and true.'

(From Harmonic Wealth by James Arthur Ray.)

As outlined earlier, to achieve true success in life not only do you measure your financial wealth, being one of the five elements to achieving 'Harmonic Wealth', but relationship wealth is also a vital strand in the equation. Life in isolation from your fellow human beings is unnatural, lonely and unfulfilled.

"I'm not time wasting....I'm boosting my recreational wealth...."

Many business people, especially the self-employed, have dedicated the best years of their lives to the creation of the enterprise and the accumulation of financial wealth. But neither time, nor investment has been directed towards relationship wealth.

If you believe that financial wealth alone can bring you happiness, contentment, a sense of fulfilment and peace of mind, then the words below are probably not for you.

If you wish to meet the perfect soul mate – firstly, become the perfect soul mate and see how easy it is to attract one. Soul mates are individuals intimately drawn to one another, through a favourable meeting of minds, and who find mutual acceptance and understanding. Soul mates may feel themselves bonded together for a lifetime.

Psychologists have suggested that all humans have a motivational drive to form and maintain caring inter-personal relationships. According to this view, people need both stable relationships and satisfying interactions with the people in those relationships. If either of these two ingredients is missing, people will begin to feel anxious, lonely, depressed, and unhappy.

SUMMARY: The lack of personal relationships can ultimately have a negative effect on your ability to conduct business and can often lead to various other abuses. It is within your grasp to rectify the situation.

CHAPTER 72
Repeat Business

The most difficult aspect of selling is to entice a potential customer to try your product or service for the first time. Billions are spent annually on achieving this objective. Unfortunately, it is often the case that the back-up service is so poor that customers vow never to repeat the business and worst of all they relate their experience to all their contacts.

"We value your call....dial 1 for annoying music, 2 for all our operators are busy, 3 for half baked excuses, 4 for....."

Some time back, my colleague was enticed to change to a new service provider for his landline phone. Several months into the contract, one of the phone numbers ceased to work. He sent messages by e-mail to the Customer Service department. He left numerous phone messages on the answering service. As a last resort, he wrote a letter to the CEO.

Over a month passed before a human representative of the company contacted him. There was no apology and he had to persevere for several more weeks to get a line rental rebate for the period that the number was out of order. The explanation for the delay was that the company had been inundated with new customers. Needless to say, at the end of his 12-month contractual period with the new company, he returned to his former provider.

SUMMARY: The old fundamentals are even more relevant today than they were during the boom years. Once you have a customer, hold on as if that was your last and only customer. An attitude of complacency and arrogance is rampant in many service providers. Instead, put yourself in your customers' shoes and see if you appreciate the experience.

CHAPTER 73
Revenge

'Retaliation for a wrongdoing.'

'Revenge is great fun: To roll over your tongue the prospect of bitter confrontations still to come, to savour to the last toothsome morsel, both the pain you are receiving and the pain you are giving back ... The chief drawback is that what you are wolfing down is yourself.'

From time to time in the cut and trust of business, you can be wronged or shafted by a colleague, friend or stranger. Seeking revenge is a natural and understandable reaction. Bill Zanker, President and founder of the very successful 'The Learning Annex' preaches the necessity to get even: 'Always fight back and get even. If you are afraid to fight back, people will think of you as a loser'.

An alternative approach is to walk away and focus all your energy on re-inventing yourself. The desire for revenge can harm you and can lead to illogical decisions and faulty strategy.

'Always forgive your enemies – nothing annoys them so much.'

(Oscar Wilde)

SUMMARY: The desire to seek revenge should be resisted on each, and every, occasion. Get on with your business and your life. Never lose your focus. The best form of revenge is success.

CHAPTER 74
Retiring Chairperson

Have a party for the departing Chairperson and invite the maximum number of employees to attend. Invite the Press. Resist his/her request to retain an office within the building. If necessary, rent an office suite at the other side of town for him/her and if s/he wishes to retain the use of a former secretary, have them re-located to the new office suite.

"..and anytime you're passing, call in for a coffee....."

SUMMARY: You could not imagine a situation where the retiring President of the USA was allowed to retain an office in the White House, or the retiring British Prime Minister retained an office in 10 Downing Street. The new person at the helm could be totally undermined by such an arrangement.

CHAPTER 75
Sales Solve All Problems

Irrespective of the business or service, the key to survival, is fundamentally sales. Without sales, there is no hope of success. The Sales policy needs to be fine-tuned to ensure that there is a positive cash flow, minimal bad debts and that each sale contributes a gross margin. It there is not a gross margin, then the activity is futile. Sales without a gross profit remind me of the saying: 'You will never be unemployed if you work for nothing.'

All sales will not produce the same gross profit, nor is that necessary. Time, and time again in Europe, and mainly as a result of the growth of Ryanair, the variation in the cost of airline tickets, on the exact same flight, can vary enormously. It is possible to fly several thousand kilometres for a single cent, plus taxes. It is not immediately obvious how the airlines actually make a profit with such a pricing policy.

In the case of Ryanair, it can expect a percentage of purchasers not to turn up, thus, the taxes and airport charges fall to the airline. Ryanair also receive significant commissions from Hertz per number of passengers landed, as opposed to the number that rent a car. There are also in-flight sales of food and beverages, lotto scratch cards, telephone discount cards and a selection of gifts. Also, Ryanair receives commissions from local tourist associations for the number of tourists landed. There are multiple opportunities for Ryanair to sell goods and services via its website, including insurance and hotel accommodation.

* * * *

The status of the sales department in many organisations is not fully recognised. It performs an essential function in providing the fuel for the business.

In the case of commercial radio, it is not unusual to find that the best-paid employees are the presenters who often take on a celebrity status. It is argued that it is the DJs that attract the listeners and that a high level of listeners is the incentive for the advertisers to buy ad space. The sales force within a radio station is not always remunerated in accordance with their contribution to the financial success of the business.

SUMMARY: Frequently, the background of the CEO is not in sales and, as such, that activity receives little direct participation from him/her. This is an error. Sales should be the primary focus of the entire organisation. All other functions should be seen as a support for sales.

CHAPTER 76
Secretaries

Judge to secretary: 'Is there any reason you could not serve as a juror in this case?'

Secretary: 'I don't want to be away from my job that long.'

Judge: 'Can't they do without you at work?'

Secretary: 'Yes, but I don't want them to know it.'

Traditionally, the boss's secretary was a young attractive female who considered her rank to be well above her station in the company's hierarchy. She was usually perched in an outer office leading into the boss's sanctum.

She had many uses. Apart from typing letters and screening phone calls, she would arrange his wife's birthday flowers and Christmas gift, his kids' birthday gifts and she would serve endless cups of coffee or tea to the boss and his visitors. She also determined which of the lower ranking executives and employees got in to speak with the boss.

The traditional secretary would be loyal, way above the call of duty, and work without extra pay, late into the night, and even at the weekends, if required to do so by the boss. She was the brunt of many jokes and viewed with some suspicion by the boss's wife. From time to time, the boss would need to take his secretary on business trips abroad. Now and again, the boss would be caught behaving inappropriately but not illegally, with the secretary.

In the more enlightened companies of today, the CEO can do his own letters, thanks to Microsoft Word, respond by e-mail and even use text services. The telephonist/receptionist can take the details of all incoming callers and state that the CEO will call back between the hours 11am to 1pm and, for the after-lunch callers, between 4pm and 6pm. The Central Support Services, which houses photocopiers, fax machines, postal franking machines and provides the 'secretarial pool' to the entire company, is a much more efficient and effective arrangement than each executive having a designated secretary.

Open access to the CEO is possible to all colleagues and if s/he is engaged, they can pop back later. By using Microsoft, the sensitive anniversaries can be logged and automatic 24-hour reminders can be issued by e-mail to the boss's I-Phone or Blackberry. Self-service tea, coffee and mineral water bars can be located conveniently for all to use. The arranging of appointments by the CEO becomes easier if s/he lifts the phone, with the 'cyber' diary open in front of him/her. Talking directly by phone to the person s/he wishes to meet results in an agreed appointment being immediately logged.

SUMMARY: The need for a secretary or PA is unnecessary. The net result will be: less late working for the CEO; no working at the weekends; no suspicious wife/husband; greater efficiency and more accessibility for his/her colleagues.

CHAPTER 77
Seven Deadly Sins

These are considered the most objectionable traits or characteristics in humans and have evolved over many centuries. They have been used from early Christian times to educate us about the obstacles we face if we want to achieve everlasting life after death.

Not only are there the seven deadly sins but there are also the seven virtues. In the business world today, has the seven deadly sins' dogma any relevance?

- **Gluttony** is the over-indulgence and over-consumption of anything, to the point of waste. The opposite being temperance.

- **Greed** is the excessive desire for material wealth. The inverse being charity.

- **Envy** is to resent that another person has something, which is perceived as lacking in you and the wish to deprive the other person of it. The inverse of envy is kindness.

- **Lust** or lechery is excessive thoughts of sexual desire which can lead to compulsions and transgressions to include sexual addiction, fornication, adultery, bestiality, rape, perversion, incest and sexual harassment. The opposite being chastity.

- **Pride** is the deadliest sin of all and is the foundation for all other deadly sins to flourish. It is the desire to be more important or attractive than others, failing to recognise the good in others and excessive self-love. It is also characterised by unjustified boasting. The inverse is humility.

- **Sloth** is the failure to utilise one's talents and gifts. The inverse being diligence.

- **Wrath** could be described as uncontrollable feelings of hatred and anger, leading to the desire for revenge and the wish to do harm or evil to others. The inverse of wrath is patience.

Tim McCormick FCA identifies seven characteristics in businesses that can ultimately lead to insolvency and liquidation. These might be summarised as:

1. Ignoring change
2. Autocratic management
3. Lack of control
4. Over-trading
5. Over-borrowing
6. Concentration of risk
7. Creative accounting

SUMMARY: The business community is a sub-group of the population. It is impossible to seek to apply 'Christian' standards in the wider population and then to accept that the business sub-group should operate on a lesser set of standards and code of conduct.

CHAPTER 78
Sexual Harassment

A woman was at work when a man said: 'Your hair smells nice.'

She went straight to her boss and said: 'I've been sexually harassed. A man said my hair smells nice.'

He replied: 'What's wrong with that, it does?'

She said: 'The man who said it was a midget.'

Sexual harassment is usually the older, male superior making unsolicited approaches towards the female junior. It is often very much a case of the male predator versus the female victim. The junior female is in a very precarious position, in that she has few options.

In the smaller organisation, there may be no procedures in place to deal with this issue and literally the only option open to the junior staff member is to leave their job and move on or risk going directly to the top of the organisation and possibly not being believed. Like bullying, the effect of sexual harassment on the victim ranges from poor physical health, mental stress, depression, insomnia and in some cases it too can lead to suicide.

In the more enlightened companies, procedures to deal with sexual harassment, and indeed all types of bullying, are set out in a code which is part of the terms and conditions of employment, clearly set out in the employee's letter of employment. The procedures for reporting and investigating are fully explained.

If it is the ultimate owner of the company that is engaged in the harassment, this poses a further problem, which may require the assistance of employment equality officers or a legal option.

"The photocopier has logged a complaint of sexual harassment"

SUMMARY: Sexual harassment is not a joke. It is very serious. Sexual harassment can and does destroy lives. Never underestimate the anxiety and distress caused by such activity. Have a proactive policy to keep all employees, including the Directors, aware that such activity, if reported, will not be swept under the carpet but will be fully investigated with appropriate sanctions employed, including dismissal, against the perpetrators.

CHAPTER 79
Shareholders' AGM

This is an annual statutory meeting of shareholders. It is usually stage-managed by the Board of Directors. They thwart dissident shareholders from getting voted onto the Board, from questioning Directors' remuneration, objecting to the audit fee and from opposing the re-appointment of rotating Directors.

It appears that only the 'little people', who have invested their own money, bother to read the annual accounts and attend the AGM.

"In lieu of an annual dividend, we're going to give each of you a ride around the block in Mr. Slocolmbe's limo."

The institutional investors appear to simply fill in the proxies to permit the Chairperson to vote, usually in favour of motions devised by that same Chairperson. It also would appear that many of these institutional investors never bother to read the financial accounts, judging by their lack of outrage at the shenanigans taking place in some of these companies.

One could be forgiven for believing that some of these institutional investors have forgotten that they are the trusted custodians and managers of millions of workers' pension contributions.

At the end of the AGM, you will usually find that the Board will host lunch for themselves, some senior managers, the invited Press, the larger shareholders, their bankers, the auditors and, especially, for the representatives from the institutional investment community, who have just arrived. Friday is a suitable day for such rituals, as the feasting can continue up to the start of the weekend, without the trouble of returning to the office.

SUMMARY: If you are a shareholder, be prepared to be ignored and gagged at the AGM. In reality and irrespective of the company's constitution, you do not have a voice. The event is regularly stage-managed to the disadvantage of the smaller shareholder.

CHAPTER 80
Solicitors

Prospective client to solicitor: 'If I give you €1,000 will you answer two questions for me?'

Solicitor's reply: 'Absolutely; what is your second question?'

The services of solicitors are essential to facilitate many aspects of a company's daily business, including: employee issues, non-paying debtors, property acquisition, other contractual issues and liability claims. To use one legal person for all of the above issues would be unwise. Specialised legal advice is often required for a particular issue, which demands the services of several solicitors.

There is no such thing as a good firm of solicitors. Solicitors are individuals. You can only judge a good solicitor as an individual, within

"There's a coincidence..I'm working on your case right now..."

the firm of solicitors by his/her commitment to providing a service. If s/he is not prepared to give you mobile and home phone numbers, s/he is unlikely to be the right person to meet your requirements. As for competence – time will be the only means of establishing that.

Avoid the celebrity solicitor who regularly appears on chat shows and the gossip columns of newspapers and magazines. This solicitor will bore the ear off you, relating the exploits of their famous clients, as a conversation piece in their local lunch venue where you are sure to be invited for the preliminary meeting. Any advice that they might give you is unlikely to be sound and definitely do not litigate on the advice of one of this Group – you are sure to lose or at best be awarded derisory damages.

Avoid the solicitor that works part-time, due to family or other commitments – when you need them they have inevitably left the office.

> **SUMMARY:** There are many good, honest and hard-working solicitors that provide an excellent service to their clients. The problem is that there are also many that are neither competent nor honest. Seek a recommendation from a respected colleague or friend.

CHAPTER 81
Sponsorship

When the mobile phone company O2 purchased the naming rights of the concert arena in Dublin, Ireland, for many millions, I immediately changed my phone provider to its competitor. The reality is that it would be I, and the other customers of O2, that would be paying for this extravaganza.

Sponsorship of high profile events is an expensive outlay and the benefits are very suspect. It is the existing customer that has to pay. Banks loved to indulge in this sort of activity, as it provided a day out at the event for the executives and a number of existing customers. What a waste!

During the famous Cheltenham horse racing festival, it was virtually impossible to get hold of a bank executive – a whole week's work was lost as they entertained existing customers at the races.

The collapse of the Celtic Tiger has brought a totally different dimension to sponsorship. It is interesting to see the sponsorship billboards that still litter the rugby and football grounds: Many of the named sponsors have since gone out of business or have had to be taken over in a State bailout.

SUMMARY: Sponsorship, is a method of advertising and, as previously discussed, most advertising is a waste of time. Sponsorship has to top the bill of wasteful expenditure and is more often fuelled by the Chairperson's or CEO's ego than any serious commercial assessment.

CHAPTER 82
Staff

The pulse of an organisation is the staff, from the highest paid to the lowest paid. All staff should be treated with the utmost dignity and respect. You do not have to pay remuneration greater than your competitor to achieve the accolade of looking after your staff.

The owner of a chain of supermarkets related a story about a touching example of a happy and satisfied staff to me:

'Jim approached his employer, the owner of the business, in October and stated that he would be of retiring age in a few weeks' time. He proposed to finish his employment at the end of November.

He recalled that he had been working for the organisation for some 29 years and stated that on each and every work day, when he awoke in the morning, he looked forward to coming in to work'.

Jim did retire that November but in early December of the same year, Jim died in his sleep. Three days later his wife of 35 years passed away.'

* * * *

There are many skills required to employ the right staff. It was said that, historically, if you turned up for a job interview in IBM in anything other than a white shirt and a smart suit you simply would not be hired.

Feargal Quinn, founder of Superquinn, the number one Irish quality supermarket chain, revealed that a pre-condition for being hired was that you had a smile on your face. And the excellent attitude and courteous response, from each, and every, member of staff, reflected that very thing.

SUMMARY: The Staff is an organisation's most important asset. With a little effort from the top, work can be an enjoyable and fulfilling experience every day. This will be reflected in reduced sick days, less industrial disputes and fewer employment tribunal appearances for the organisation.

It is very simple – treat the staff as you would like to be treated. They too wish to go home in the evening with a sense of achievement and having contributed to the company, and to enjoy the rest of the day with their families and friends. They too wish to have healthcare and educate their children and to look forward to some financial security in the future when they retire.

CHAPTER 83
Staff Training

It might be fashionable to send staff off to outside organisations for training but it is likely to be expensive and is unlikely to achieve a fraction of what was promised in the brochure.

The best staff training is on the job. Avoid all types of 'encounter group' training, which entails reporting to 'facilitators'. These are outsiders who do not know your business and you end up paying them to interrogate your staff. In this type of staff training, the business world becomes artificial. There are deep probing questions like: 'Where would you like to be within the organisation, five years from now?' This is a total waste of time. Can you imagine paying someone to carry this out?

At one such session, the facilitator asked the attendees to close their eyes and imagine a scene whereby a storm brought flooding, destruction, havoc, death and suffering to a particular community. At the end of the description the participants were asked to write a single word, giving their immediate response to the scenario. All but one of the participants' responses was about feelings of desperation, sadness and hopelessness. The non-empathetic response, from a single participant, was the word 'opportunity'.

The facilitator was very impressed by such a response, seeing it as sign of future leadership qualities.

When asked to expand on his answer, the attendee replied: 'With so much confusion and destruction, there is an opportunity to take advantage and to exploit the stricken community.'

SUMMARY: Staff training is important, not only on the technical aspects of the employee's job but also on the ethos of the company. In particular, the company's desire to look after the customer and improve their experience needs to be continuously reinforced. Staff training also needs to address the issues of bullying and sexual harassment. Usually the best and most appropriate staff training is in-house and on the job.

CHAPTER 84
Starting A Business

A young businessman had just started his own firm. He rented a smart office suite and had it furnished with antiques. Sitting there, he saw a man come into the outer office. Wishing to appear the hot-shot, the businessman picked up the phone and started to pretend he had a big deal working.

He threw huge figures around and made giant commitments. Finally he hung up and asked the visitor: 'Can I help you?'

The man said: 'Yeah, I've come to activate your phone lines.'

There is no such thing as the right time to start a business. It's like getting married, or having children or buying your first house. You just get on with it. It is a gamble, irrespective of the research that you put into it prior to getting started.

You can be guaranteed that you will work longer hours than the average Japanese worker, age faster, worry more and often wonder why you did not stick to the secure 9-5, Monday to Friday, boring old job, with your carefree colleagues.

Your projections will be over-optimistic and you can expect turnover to be six months later kicking in and 50% lower than the projections. The debtor days will be 90 instead of the 45 days set out in the projections. If you need some bank borrowings, please confirm that you have clearly understood and implemented the bit of common sense that is at hand on the previous pages, under the heading 'Bank Borrowings'.

A little input on some basic book-keeping and accounting may require the assistance of a young accountant, who is also starting out in business and is hungry to assist. Ideally the accountant should be within walking distance of your base and unless s/he is prepared to give you a personal mobile number and home number, s/he is the wrong person for you.

Start out with the minimum of expenses and, if possible, work out of your home initially. Only hire your first staff member when you know exactly what is entailed in that function and that you are already fully competent in its performance. If you do not, you will not only be unable to evaluate his/her performance but you will also be a prisoner to his/her knowledge and expertise. Stay small until you are on top of all aspects of the operation.

SUMMARY: If at all possible, start your business as a 'nixer' or an 'extra' or 'side line' whilst still an employee. When the 'side line' starts to produce a positive cash flow and remaining an employee is not in harmony with growing the business, then resign. At least you will have gained the start-up experience, with the security of the monthly pay cheque still covering your day-to-day outlays.

CHAPTER 85
Suggestion Boxes

Within every organisation in the world there lurks untapped talent in the management and work force that is bubbling with new ideas. They have suggestions from how to cut back on outlays and waste, to creative ideas and profit contributors.

Engaging with this resource is regularly ignored. The long established suggestion box is growing cobwebs from non-utilisation and the line mangers are the worst people to carry ideas from colleagues to senior managers. Employees also do not wish to look stupid and are often unable to articulate by written submission, hence the waste of the suggestion box.

"Your suggestion...'DOWNSIZING: The Only Way to Survive Recession' was of unsurpassed brilliance, it made me face reality. Your severance package will be ready first thing in the morning!"

Introduce a widely published profit-sharing scheme whereby the originator gets a financial reward, based on the return to the company, from implementation of the idea. Have the line managers organise 'idea' sessions, with the authority to immediately introduce good ideas that fall within a €10,000 cost budget.

For employees who are happy to email their ideas to the CEO, introduce an 'ideas@boss.com' address, which will only be read by the CEO. S/he can forward the idea to the line manager, not accredited if required, and wait for the manager to take action.

Mikhail Kalashnikov began his armaments' career while he was in a hospital, after being wounded in battle in 1941. As a 'hobby weapon designer', he began by tinkering with a sub-machine gun design.

Kalashnikov designed a carbine, strongly influenced by the American M1 Garand. At the same time, the Soviet Army was interested in developing a true assault rifle. Eventually, by 1946, the Kalashnikov AK-1 was created. Subsequently, it was one of his most junior assistants, Aleksandr Zaytsev, who meekly suggested a major re-design of the AK-1, to improve reliability. The modified rifle was produced and shown to be simple and reliable, under a wide range of conditions, with convenient handling characteristics. In 1949 it was adopted by the Soviet Army.

Today the Kalashnikov is still the most commonly used assault rifle in the world, with its annual production out-stripping the combined total for all other assault rifles.

SUMMARY: Create a platform to tap into the ideas and knowledge of your employees. Create an enthusiasm amongst the staff to cut down on waste, achieve greater efficiency and promote new ideas. Monetary rewards are the best incentive.

CHAPTER 86
Tax Avoidance

'The Eiffel Tower is Canary Wharf after taxes.'

'Over and over again Courts have said there is nothing sinister in so arranging one's affairs as to keep taxes as low as possible. Everybody does so, rich and poor, and all do right, for nobody owes any public duty to pay more than the law demands. Taxes are enforced extractions, not voluntary contributions. To demand more in the name of morals is mere cant.'

(Honourable Learned Hand, US Appeals Court Justice)

Fundamentally there are two ways to reduce your tax bill. The first method is the use of tax avoidance schemes. These are either provided for directly, by way of specific legislation, or are schemes that are devised by highly creative tax advisers which seek to place an interpretation on legislation that was not intended by the authors.

"Wait a minute! Aren't you the accountant I fired last year?"

The Revenue Service usually accepts both types of tax avoidance, albeit with the possibility of a 'look-back' audit that may declare the creative schemes to be artificial and not allowable. This will result in the 'avoided' tax having to be paid and possibly some penalties being levied. If the scheme is highly creative, it is better to flag it clearly to the Revenue at the time of its introduction. This can mitigate penalties, if it is declared unacceptable at a later date.

The second way to reduce your tax is by tax evasion, which is simply illegal. It is deliberately breaking the law by not reporting taxable income, capital gains or transactions giving rise to stamp duty or other taxes. The use of foreign bank accounts has played an essential role in facilitating this crime. However, with the increased efforts, and necessity, to track down the financing of terrorism and the money laundering of the proceeds of drug trafficking, human trafficking and general organised crime, the authorities in the UK, USA and Ireland have tripped across large scale tax evasion.

This has resulted in untold misery, sleepless nights and, in certain cases, imprisonment for tax cheats who were caught. In many instances the ultimate cost has exceeded three times the amount of the original tax concealed.

* * * *

'The art of taxation consists in so plucking the goose as to get the most feathers, with the least hissing.'

In 2008, an economic scandal in Germany was triggered when an employee of a Liechtenstein bank, LGT Bank, sold a DVD to the German Government. The DVD implicated as many as 900 wealthy Germans in a tax evasion scandal, with the massive amounts involved estimated to be in the region of €4 billion.

Deutsche Post CEO, Klaus Zumwinkel, was the first tax cheat to have a public outing. He was forced to resign in February 2008 after tax officials raided his home and office looking for evidence of massive tax evasion.

The source of the DVD was paid €5 million by the German authorities and was granted anonymity and personal protection. Several thousand LGT Bank customers are thought to be compromised by the information, which remains in the hands of the German investigators. It has now been revealed that the Germans have also obtained account information from another Bank, Liechtensteinische Landesbank (LLB), which has highlighted further tax evasion.

The growing scandal has caused outrage across the country. German Chancellor, Angela Merkel, again reminded German commercial and economic leaders that they carry a huge responsibility: 'Responsible behaviour from companies is an elementary pre-requisite for a functioning, socially-responsible, market economy.'

The political parties have also accused the wealthy in Germany of ignoring the responsibility they have for the common good. One politician commented: 'The money that perpetrators keep from the community short-changes education, security and infrastructure.'

* * * *

Q. What is the difference between a terrorist and a tax inspector?

A. You can negotiate with a terrorist.

In the UK, according to HM Revenue & Customs, Britain's tax collecting body, the Chancellor of the Exchequer will recover around £70 million of lost taxes – and possibly as much as £100 million – annually. This is a direct result of the EU savings directive, which came into force in July 2005. It makes it harder for investors to keep quiet about off-shore savings accounts, in which British bank customers hold an estimated £10 billion. At least, that was the figure until the introduction of the rules which caused a flurry of activity from savers who moved up to £500 million back to accounts in the UK or to tax havens further afield, such as Dubai and Singapore.

* * * *

A professor of taxation delivers a highly-detailed, brilliant lecture, drawing the distinction between tax avoidance and tax evasion. He then asks his brightest student: 'Tell us succinctly what the difference is between tax avoidance and tax evasion.'

The student replies: 'Jail.'

SUMMARY: There is ample evidence that people who have participated in tax evasion activities will not enjoy the fruits of their crime. The positive approach to taxation is to focus on earning more, so that you can comfortably pay your taxation and still have a significant amount of money left at your disposal.

CHAPTER 87
Tipping

A man was eating a meal at a restaurant. He checks his pockets and leaves his tip – three pennies. As he strides toward the door, his waitress muses, only half to herself:

'You know, you can tell a lot about a man by the tip he leaves.'

The man turns around, curiosity getting the better of him.: 'Oh, really? Tell me, what my tip says?'

'Well, this penny tells me you're a thrifty man.'

Barely able to conceal his pride, the man utters: 'Hmm, true enough.'

'And this penny, it tells me you're a bachelor.'

Surprised at her perception, he says: 'Well, that's true, too.'

'And the third penny tells me that your father was one, too.'

* * * *

A gratuity is a special financial thank you from the customer to the individual serving you. It is discretionary and is over and above the price of the product and service being provided. Tipping is traditional in the hospitality industry and, to a lesser extent, in the taxi trade. Where there is a service charge, your discretion is being removed, so do not add another tip on top of that charge.

From time to time, it is amusing to observe the positive and helpful attitude that arises from staff, just as you are about to request your bill. You have been treated like an inconvenience since you arrived but then, towards the end of your visit, the staff starts to 'cosy up' to you. Be polite, thank them and demonstrate your lack of appreciation by leaving no tip. If the suggested or discretionary tip is applied to the bill, ask to have it removed. Hopefully the message will go out to the staff that tips are for service that is above the call of duty and not a right.

On a recent visit to the USA, the waitress had been most efficient, courteous and helpful, from the moment our party arrived at the restaurant. Recognising that I was European, she announced, prior to my request for the bill, that in America tipping was 15% of the amount of the bill. As she explained Europeans would not be familiar with this tradition.

As I settled the bill, plus a 10% tip, I respectfully suggested that in Europe the menu prices were the contractual obligation and anything above that was discretionary and that I had no reason to think that anything different could apply in the USA

> **SUMMARY:** There is a form of intimidation in operation in some restaurants about the gratuity. A tip is a special thank you. If you have been treated well and have enjoyed the experience, absolutely leave a tip. If you have not enjoyed the experience, leave no tip.

CHAPTER 88
Trade Unions

Negotiations between union members and their employer were at an impasse. The union denied that the workers were flagrantly abusing their contracts' sick-leave provisions.

One morning at the bargaining table, the company's chief negotiator held aloft the morning edition of the newspaper. 'This man,' he announced, 'called in sick yesterday!' There, on the sports page, was a photo of the supposedly ill employee, winning a local golf tournament, with an excellent score.

A union negotiator broke the silence in the room. 'Wow,' he said. 'Think of what kind of score he could have had if he hadn't been sick!'

* * * *

Trade Unions emerged as a reaction to the exploitation of workers who were often working in very poor and dangerous conditions, for long hours, at very low pay.

In today's modern economy, unions still exist and whilst there are still some instances of workers' rights being violated unions, largely, have had a very negative impact on the modern economy. Workers entering certain industries have no real option other than to join the union, otherwise they are ostracised by colleagues.

Within those industries where they hold power, unions have objected to the most modest attempts at progress. In Dublin, the bus workers' union was in negotiations for 27 years before the employer got agreement to introduce driver-only buses and to stop hiring the fare conductor. The fact that the union could delay the employer for such a long period of time may also indicate that the company had poor leadership.

Again in Dublin, for years the taxi unions had a veto on the number of new licenses being issued. It was not unusual to spend more than an hour waiting for a taxi and late at night the waiting time could extend to up to three hours. Existing taxi permits were a tradable commodity and sold for a price equating to approximately four years' turnover. In 2002, it was a brave Government Minister, Bobby Molloy, from the minority coalition party that removed the cap of approximately 3,000 licenses. Within the next 12 months the number of permits applied for and granted exceeded 12,000. The taxi unions proceeded to go on strike, by blocking the city's main road system, causing untold misery and hardship to many. The strike was in vain. The union bosses misread the public mood.

In the depths of the 2008–2010 recession, the union representing the Air Traffic Controllers brought Ireland to a standstill in January 2010 so its members could attend a mandatory four hour union meeting. Behind this meeting was a growing dispute. The union had instructed its members not to co-operate with the implementation of new software and new technology, whilst it attempted to negotiate a 6% pay increase. The air traffic controllers are some of the best paid employees in Ireland.

The unions throughout Europe and the USA have obstructed change. This has led directly to many millions of jobs being transferred to Asia. As the first decade of the new millennium comes to an end, the world economic landscape has changed in favour of the Asian work force.

SUMMARY: In many instances trade unions have lost the moral high ground. They are seen as being too conditioned to demand more reward for their members, for less work, to resist change and to encourage demarcation. Trade Unions and in particular some senior officials, appear to have a very negative and anti-business agenda, which does not serve members' interests well in the longer term. The role and future of the Trade Unions are limited in the modern, enlightened company. There is now adequate labour legislation protecting workers' rights. Generally, there is the perception that it is the disgruntled, lazy and inefficient employees who whip up discontent.

CHAPTER 89
Trust

In days of old, when knights were bold, a particular Knight was leaving on a crusade. He called his squire: 'I'm leaving for the crusade. Here is the key to my wife's chastity belt. If, in five years I have not returned, you may use the key as I am sure that she will have needs.'

The Knight sets out down the road, fully armoured. He takes one last look back towards his castle and sees the squire rushing across the drawbridge, shouting: 'Halt! Halt! Thank goodness I was able to catch up with you. This is the wrong key!'

Never be tempted to be in business or even to do business with someone whom you do not trust. The fundamental for all relationships is trust. Once you have satisfied yourself that you trust the prospective partner, customer or supplier, secure the relationship in strong, legal agreements or other controls. Never apologise for this exercise. Outline it up front.

Equally the person who states that you can trust them is to be avoided like the plague.

The same principal also applies to all of your employees – you must be able to trust them. Having established that much implement proper and appropriate internal controls, if for no other reason, than to prevent them from being tempted into fraudulent activity.

The most unusual contract that you will ever enter is that of marriage. You marry for love; Trust is totally mutual. However, your marriage certificate is all about financial rights, duties, inheritances, property and custody of children. It does not say that on the certificate. But it is there. It is a legally, binding contract and the only matter not covered by it is love itself.

When love fades and a break up becomes inevitable, you will never see so much anger, passion, revenge, mistrust and hatred as that between the two former, intimate friends who had earlier promised a life partnership. The legal battle will be more emotional and vicious than any business battle. Logic will simply not apply. It is the perfect reason to have a prenuptial agreement but you must be careful in which jurisdiction you execute it.

* * * *

The former Beatle Paul McCartney joined in matrimony with Heather Mills in June 2002, after the untimely death of Linda, his wife of many years. Being romantic and trusting, it was common currency that Paul did not execute a prenuptial agreement with Heather. The perfect match lasted a few short years. As the marriage fell apart, Heather launched a full public assault for sympathy and money, with claims of mental torture against Paul.

The press sided with the highly popular and respected former Beatle. Endless stories were printed, with allegations of sexual permissiveness against Heather, in her alleged former career as a high class prostitute.

Subsequently, in March 2008, Justice Bennett ruled on the divorce settlement and stated that Heather Mills' evidence was inconsistent and inaccurate, while that of Paul McCartney was honest. Whilst Paul got away with a minimal settlement of circa £24 million, the lack of a prenuptial agreement created many months of unwanted publicity and a loss of privacy for both parties.
So much for trust.

A woman was in bed with her husband's best friend when the phone rang. After hanging up, she turned to her lover and said: 'That was Bernard, but don't worry, he won't be home for a while. He's playing cards with you.'

SUMMARY: In business, the greater the charm the more valid the mistrust. Endless landowners have been cruelly cheated out of a fair value for their property by some of the unscrupulous property developers that lived the 'Celtic Tiger Dream'. Do not be taken in by sweet talk. Always be on your guard.

The End

And finally, we have run out of diesel. We would appreciate if you would take the time to send us your comments, views and contributions. Any that are inserted in the next edition shall be acknowledged.

Kind regards,

Rory & Gerry

rorycarron@gmail.com